MW00824482

THE FOOD AND COOKING OF
ESTONIA, LATVIA AND LITHUANIA

THE FOOD AND COOKING OF
ESTONIA, LATVIA AND LITHUANIA

traditions · ingredients · tastes · techniques · over 60 classic recipes

SILVENA JOHAN LAUTA

Photography by Martin Brigdale

This edition is published by Aquamarine

Aquamarine is an imprint of
Anness Publishing Ltd
Hermes House, 88–89 Blackfriars Road,
London SE1 8HA
tel. 020 7401 2077; fax 020 7633 9499

www.aquamarinebooks.com
www.annesspublishing.com

If you like the images in this book and want
to investigate using them for publishing,
promotions or advertising, please visit our
website www.practicalpictures.com for
more information.

UK agent: The Manning Partnership Ltd;
tel. 01225 478444; fax 01225 478440;
sales@manning-partnership.co.uk

UK distributor: Grantham Book Services
Ltd; tel. 01476 541080; fax 01476 541061;
orders@gbs.tbs-ltd.co.uk

North American agent/distributor: National
Book Network; tel. 301 459 3366; fax 301
429 5746; www.nbnbooks.com

Australian agent/distributor: Pan Macmillan
Australia; tel. 1300 135 113; fax 1300 135
103; customer.service@macmillan.com.au

New Zealand agent/distributor: David
Bateman Ltd; tel. (09) 415 7664; fax (09)
415 8892

Publisher: Joanna Lorenz
Editorial Director: Helen Sudell
Project Editor: Emma Clegg
Designer: Abby Franklin
Photography: Martin Brigdale
Home economist: Fergal Connolly
Stylist: Helen Trent
Production Controller: Claire Rae

ETHICAL TRADING POLICY
Because of our ongoing ecological
investment programme, you, as our
customer, can have the pleasure and
reassurance of knowing that a tree is being
cultivated on your behalf to naturally
replace the materials used to make the
book you are holding. For further
information about this scheme, go to
www.annesspublishing.com/trees

© Anness Publishing Ltd 2009

All rights reserved. No part of this
publication may be reproduced, stored in a
retrieval system, or transmitted in any way
or by any means, electronic, mechanical,
photocopying, recording or otherwise,
without the prior written permission of the
copyright holder.

A CIP catalogue record for this book is
available from the British Library.

PUBLISHER'S NOTE
Although the advice and information in this
book are believed to be accurate and true
at the time of going to press, neither the
authors nor the publisher can accept any
legal responsibility or liability for any errors
or omissions that may be made nor for any
inaccuracies nor for any harm or injury that
comes about from following instructions or
advice in this book.

NOTES
Bracketed terms are intended for
American readers.

For all recipes, quantities are given in
both metric and imperial measures and,
where appropriate, in standard cups
and spoons. Follow one set of measures,
but not a mixture, because they are
not interchangeable.

Standard spoon and cup measures are
level. 1 tsp = 5ml, 1 tbsp = 15ml,
1 cup = 250ml/8fl oz.

Australian standard tablespoons are 20ml.
Australian readers should use 3 tsp in place
of 1 tbsp for measuring small quantities.

American pints are 16fl oz/2 cups.
American readers should use
20fl oz/2.5 cups in place of 1 pint when
measuring liquids.

Electric oven temperatures in this book are
for conventional ovens. When using a fan
oven, the temperature will probably need to
be reduced by about 10–20°C/20–40°F.
Since ovens vary, you should check with
your manufacturer's instruction book
for guidance.

The nutritional analysis given for each
recipe is calculated per portion (i.e. serving
or item), unless otherwise stated. If the
recipe gives a range, such as Serves 4–6,
then the nutritional analysis will be for the
smaller portion size, i.e. 6 servings.
Measurements for sodium do not include
salt added to taste.

Medium (US large) eggs are used unless
otherwise stated.

Front cover shows Estonian Sour Cream
and Dill Pancakes – for recipe, see
page 51.

Contents

The Baltic regions

On the eastern edge of the Baltic Sea lie the three proudly independent countries of Lithuania, Latvia and Estonia. These three countries, which have a similar geography and climate and also a shared history, are labelled 'the Baltic States'. They are tucked into the fertile, low-lying ground between the massive bulk of Russia to the north-east and Poland to the south, with Belarus on their eastern border and the chilly, shallow Baltic Sea forming the western boundary. With forests covering approximately half the land, the population density across these countries is low.

Lithuania: a temperate zone

The southernmost of the three Baltic States, Lithuania has the warmest climate, said to fall between oceanic and continental. The 'Baltic Southerners' of Lithuania are said to be more open, talkative and temperamental than their neighbours, perhaps something to do with the hotter summers and opportunities for socializing outdoors in the cafés and restaurants of the capital, Vilnius, and other towns.

Lithuania consists mainly of lowlands, criss-crossed by rivers and dotted with lakes. These waters are full of freshwater fish such as carp and pike, both typical delicacies in all the Eastern European countries, from Poland, through the Baltic States, and to Russia. The highest point in Lithuania, the Aukštojas Hill, is barely 300 metres (333 yards) high. This means that vast areas of the country are ideal for agriculture, with plenty of water for irrigation. Cereals are grown on a grand scale, particularly in the inland region of Suvalkija, with large fields stretching into the distance. Cattle and pigs graze here too, supplying the local population with plentiful dairy products and meat. Almost half of this delightfully verdant country's land area is given over to permanent agricultural use, with fields of potatoes, sugar beets and other vegetables, as well as the ubiquitous grains such as rye, barley and wheat.

The weather is changeable but reasonably mild most of the year, with average temperatures in July of 17°C (63°F), and -5°C (23°F) in January.

Below Since the country's independence, Vilnius, the capital of Lithuania, has emerged as a modern European city.

Below Dunes forming part of the Curonian Spit stretch from the south to the northern tip of Lithuania, near the port city of Klaipòda.

Right The Baltic States are located in north-central Europe, on the eastern side of the Baltic Sea, and along the western border of Russia and Belarus.

The coastline of Lithuania is short – a mere 60 miles (97km) of cold Baltic shoreline. This includes the Curonian Spit, a peninsula with sand dunes and pinewoods along its length, and home to many species of indigenous wildlife, such as the serotine bat and the grey seal. Herring and other fish are caught along this shoreline, and the natural amber blown into the shallow coastal waters is collected and carved into beautiful jewellery and ornaments.

Pine forests abound in the southern part of Lithuania known as Dzūkija, and here the tree cover of the ancient forest gives protection to the local wildlife, particularly deer, foxes and wild boar. Forest food includes beautiful wild cranberries, a local favourite in both savoury recipes, such as cranberry and apple soup, and sweet treats such as buttermilk and berry pancakes.

Vilnius – a vibrant and historic city

The capital city of Lithuania, Vilnius nestles in a picturesque river valley in the far east of the country. The historic centre is spectacular, and is a UNESCO world heritage site, featuring a well-preserved baroque old town that is fringed by the Vilnia and Neris rivers. In the old town, a mass of church spires reach for the sky; but on the north bank of the Neris, a new Vilnius is taking shape, a 21st-century collage of glass and steel skyscrapers. The city has a large student population and is also becoming a popular tourist destination, as the local beers are so tasty, especially when accompanied by a plate of fried pork and potatoes.

Latvia: a blend of north and south

Sitting squarely in the middle of the Baltic States, Latvia is the middle of the Baltic sandwich, with chilly Nordic Estonia to the north and milder Lithuania to the south. Russia and Belarus adjoin the eastern end, while the western end gives onto the Baltic Sea and then Sweden.

Although the summers can be pleasantly warm and the climate is generally ideal for agriculture, the winters can be quite harsh, and the winds from Latvia's north-eastern neighbour, Russia, nearly always brings a covering of snow from December to March. Much of the coastline, however, is slightly less exposed than the Lithuanian shores, with the capital city of Riga well protected from the cold Baltic Sea in the southern corner of the shallow Gulf of Riga.

Most of Latvia is low-lying, covered with fertile plains where pastureland for pigs and cattle meets fields of grain. There are widespread forests, remnants of the primeval forest that covered Eastern Europe. These shelter the larger species of wild game such as deer and boar, and even the edible dormouse. Rivers full of wildlife meander through the country, expanding into lakes, particularly in the hilly west, before emptying into the Baltic Sea.

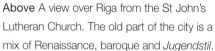
Above A view over Riga from the St John's Lutheran Church. The old part of the city is a mix of Renaissance, baroque and *Jugendstil*.

Historically, there are four distinct regions of Latvia. The northernmost area, Vidzeme, includes Riga, and other thriving cities as well as national parks and medieval castles. Along its undulating coastline and riverbanks, centuries of erosion have made spectacular sandstone cliffs and caves. Kurzeme and Zemgale are the southernmost regions, stretching from the Baltic to the Belorussian border, with ancient fishing villages in Kurzeme on the coast, where the locals still ply their trade and herring and cod are smoked. The south-eastern region, Zemgale, is Latvia's breadbasket, with the most fertile soil. Cattle and pigs thrive in these flatlands, and storks nest here every year. Latgale in the north-east is a sparsely populated region of wild landscapes and villages where the people still speak the old Latgalian dialect.

Above A winter landscape in Gaizinkalns National Park, located in the central Latvian town of Siguld.

Riga – a 21st-century capital city
The city of Riga is the geographical and business heart of the Baltic States, and a focus for education and science. Images of Communist deprivations are dispelled by a stroll around the city, with its gleaming renovated buildings, its fashion-conscious youth and many new bars and cafés. The Old Town tumbles towards the banks of the Daugava River in a maze of cobbled streets, with numerous church spires and imposing squares. Four Zeppelin hangars were moved to a site near the Daugava River and they now house the city market. Here stalls sell fresh fruit and vegetables, meat and live fish.

Estonia: a northern outlook
The most northerly of the Baltic States, Estonia is the smallest, in both land area and population. The long, wriggling

coastline looks far more Scandinavian than that of its southern neighbours, with a multitude of little inlets resembling the fjords of Norway, and a scattering of islands out in the Baltic Sea. The two largest islands are Saaremaa and Hiiumaa and are favourite holiday destinations. The intricate coastline and numerous islands are ideal places for a migratory stopover for Arctic ducks and geese, as well as other birds, and bird-watching has become a real focus. One characteristic shared with the other Baltic States is the low-lying nature of the land – at 318 metres (1,043 feet), Suur Munamägi (Egg Mountain) near the southern Latvian border is the highest point – which again makes it ideal for agricultural production.

Lake Peipsi, a huge lake, covers much of the eastern border with Russia. This is one of the best places in Europe to catch freshwater fish such as pike and bream, and commercial fishermen, local anglers and tourists alike enjoy fantastic catches.

Above Man fishing in a lake in the city of Talsi in the Kurzeme region of Latvia.

Below Gull migration in Lake Peipsi, Estonia, the fourth largest freshwater lake in Europe.

This is a thickly forested country, with almost half of the land made of up woodlands containing an amazing mixture of trees, from evergreen conifers to the deciduous broad-leaved oak and maple. The rest of the countryside consists of arable land, pasture and more than 1,400 lakes. Pigs and cattle are the favourite livestock, but the farmers also raise sheep here, because they are capable of surviving the harsh winters. Lamb dishes such as lamb shanks with sour sauce give a real flavour of Estonia and are not found so often in Latvia or Lithuania.

The summers are cool and the winters can be very cold, with the temperature rarely rising above freezing from the middle of November right through to March in the inland areas. Proximity to the Baltic Sea and the gulfs of Riga and Finland keeps the climate more moderate in the coastal parts. July and August are the wettest months, but the lakes rise and the rivers often flood in spring, a combination of rain and melting snow.

Tallinn – a medieval wonder

The capital city of Estonia, Tallinn has a population of less than half a million. This is a medieval Hanseatic seaport that sits on the Gulf of Finland at the northerly tip of Estonia. The medieval Old Town boasts a town wall with 26 defence towers and many other spectacular buildings. The Old Town is a vibrant, living organism located between the harbour and the new business district. The city centre with its cosy cafés, boutiques and art galleries beckons the visitor to take a stroll and explore the streets, to have a drink – beer in the summer and mulled wine in the winter – and a bite to eat at one of the many delightful pavement cafés. Tourists swarm in from all across Europe but in particular from Britain and from Finland.

Below Tallinn is a sea coast capital with a beautifully preserved medieval city. It is still a strong port and a thriving industrial centre.

The history of the Baltics

Because of their geographical position between eastern and western Europe, Estonia, Latvia and Lithuania have a history of frequent invasion, a factor that defines the history of the area and the psychology and culture of its people. In the 21st century, the three countries of the Baltic States no longer fear the warring countries of Europe or the mighty power of Russia. They are proud members of the EU, and independent parliamentary democracies with their own cultures and traditions. They are also deeply protective of their food heritage and its varied influences.

Early history
Estonia, Latvia and Lithuania are part of the landmass that was formed as the great glaciers of the Ice Age retreated in about 10,000BC. The fertile soil and thick forests that grew up in this corner of Europe were ripe for the development of grain and meat farming, and rich in natural resources such as coal, oil and amber. Over the centuries the three countries have been invaded by Russia, Germany, Sweden, Denmark and Poland.

Christianity came late to these countries, about the end of the 12th century, with German traders bringing Christian missionaries. These met with great resistance, and the region was not fully converted until late in the 14th century. Even then, two distinct branches of Christianity developed giving a clear distinction to the different regions – Lutherans in the north and Catholics in the south.

Fighting over trade routes
In the 16th century, the Baltic economy boomed. Unfortunately this led to more invasions from surrounding countries, especially Russia, which planned to forge a pathway to the Baltic Sea and the trading opportunities this offered with all the European nations farther west, as well as making use of the local natural resources and farming expertise. By the 19th century, much of the Baltic territory was under Russian or German rule.

Turmoil in the 20th century
World War I brought misery to the region as territorial rights ebbed and flowed between the Germans and Russians. But in 1918, Lithuania, Estonia and Latvia claimed independence, securing their rights in 1920. This period of independence was to prove short-lived.

On 23 August 1939, the Soviet Union and Germany signed a treaty of non-aggression, with a secret protocol concerning the division of Eastern Europe into spheres of influence, the 'Molotov–Ribbentrop Pact'. On 15 June 1940, the day that the German army marched into Paris, the Red Army finally occupied Lithuania. The occupation of Latvia and Estonia came soon afterwards.

What followed has become known as the 'year of terror', involving the wholesale nationalization of farming land and industry, and the deporting of local teachers, scientists and intelligentsia in cattle wagons to Siberia, where most of

Left Charles XII leading the Swedish army to victory over the Russians in 1700 at the Battle of Narva. This town was near St Petersburg in Russia and is now part of Estonia.

Above Lithuanian peasants in Sunday dress, taken in the early part of the 20th century.

Above St Stanislaus Cathedral in Vilnius has sculptures of St Casimir, St Stanislaus and St Helena on its roof, originally added in 1792. They symbolize Lithuania, Poland, and Russia.

them perished. Worse came when the declaration of war between Germany and the Soviet Union brought a rapid invasion of the Baltic States by German armed forces. Anyone who did not cooperate with the new occupation was killed or sent to concentration camps. Hundreds of thousands of Jews were also rounded up and slaughtered. But in 1944, with Nazi Germany under threat on both western and eastern fronts, the Soviet Army crossed back into the Baltic States.

The Russians imposed a tyrannical regime with strict repressive measures, persecuting those who had cooperated with Germans, or who had supported the resistance movement against the Soviets. In 1949 hundreds of thousands of Latvians, Lithuanians and Estonians were deported to Siberia, though many fled to the forests to form a resistance army.

The USSR sent a massive wave of immigrants to man their expanding manufacturing complexes. Local agricultural, religious, language and cultural traditions were discouraged; the land was nationalized and turned over to the collective farms, so a rural way of life that had survived for centuries was threatened, and a movement towards the cities soon followed.

A hard-won independence

Liberalization began within the USSR communist regime in the mid-1980s, led by Mikhail Gorbachev. At the same time as the Soviet Union began to unravel, the call came from all three Baltic States for their independence.

On 23 August 1989, 50 years after the signing of the Molotov–Ribbentrop Pact, all three Baltic countries held an amazing political demonstration which has become known as the 'Baltic Way'. The people of Estonia, Latvia and Lithuania made a human chain of two million people that stretched unbroken for 600 kilometres (nearly 400 miles) from Tallinn in the far north of Estonia, through Riga in central Latvia, to Vilnius in the south of Lithuania. This was a symbolic demonstration of the Baltic population's united will for independence.

By 1991 the independence of the Baltic States was recognized by Moscow, and the last of the Russian armed forces left in August 1994. Latvia, Lithuania and Estonia were free.

The European Union

Only a few years after gaining their independence from the former Soviet Union, the three Baltic States voted overwhelmingly to join the EU. Latvia, Lithuania and Estonia became full members on 1 May 2004, as well as members of NATO. The Baltic States are now heading to adopt the euro as their currency in 2010.

Traditional Baltic festivals

Pagan and Christian merge together in a wonderful panoply of celebrations throughout the year in the Baltic regions. Many of the colourful festivals revolve around growing food, the harvests, good health, hospitality and fertility. Eggs are brightly decorated for Easter and the colours of flowers in the midsummer celebrations emphasize the positivity and joy that runs through the festivals. There is even a celebration, called St Matthew's Day, that marks the shift to a lighter springtime diet.

Above Stalls and crowds at the Kaziuko Mugė (St Casimir Fair) before Easter on Pilies Gatvė in Vilnius, Lithuania.

St Matthew's Day

Traditionally, the first hints of spring begin around 24 February, so this is the day when the Balts mark the end of the heavier winter diet and look forward to lighter meals. Potatoes and cabbage are avoided from this date until the autumn.

St Mary's Day

On 25 March, St Mary's Day, Estonians traditionally cook large crêpes, which are eaten because it is believed that this ensures a good cabbage harvest.

Mardi Gras

Shrove Tuesday (Vastlapäev in Estonia) is Mardi Gras, a day of indulgence. The Estonians traditionally believed that eating pig's feet on this day would ensure fat healthy pigs in the coming months and, as this belief was so common, the day also became known as Pig's Feet Holiday. Eating peas and beans was also supposed to encourage the pea and bean crops. Another custom was to eat cream-filled rolls flavoured with a hint of rosewater, to ensure good-quality livestock. All these customs are still followed.

Easter and spring

Pagan spring celebrations and Christian traditions are combined at Easter, so the whole of the Easter week (Lihavõtted in Estonia), between Palm Sunday and Easter Sunday, is a special occasion.

All across the Baltic States eggs are brightly decorated and placed in bowls or baskets to set on a table spread with a white tablecloth decorated with spring flowers and grasses. Foods enjoyed for the celebrations are pork, veal, chicken, potato and beetroot (beet) salads, cold meats, fish, sausages, cheeses and egg dishes. Sauerkraut is not eaten on Palm Sunday, as it is considered to be bad luck, but it is eaten at other times over Easter. On Easter afternoon children will visit their godparents and neighbours to receive Easter eggs as gifts.

When spring arrives Latvian people hang swings from trees to swing on. They say that if you can swing high, the grain will grow high, but make sure that no unpleasant thoughts enter your head while you are swinging. To help you, you must carry an egg to ward off such thoughts. If you bury an egg under the swing it will help to protect you from evil for the whole year. There are other fertility traditions that go with the swing: if a man throws an egg over the swing and catches it on the other side, then he will have a wife; if he is already married, then he will have a child.

Midsummer

The biggest party in the Baltic calendar takes place at midsummer, beginning on the night of 23 June and spilling over into the following morning. This modern-day celebration with eating, drinking and dancing harks back to a pagan tradition with magic and mystery that has survived everything from Christianity to Soviet occupation. It is considered to be one of the most important holidays, even rivalling Christmas.

The entire festival is focused on nature, birth, growth and fertility, marking the change in the farming cycle from the spring sowing and planting to the summer reaping, harvesting and hay-making.

There are many ancient traditions that are still practised. Most importantly, bonfires are lit to frighten away mischievous spirits and thus ensure a good harvest. One ancient tradition saw young couples who were soon to be married jumping over the fire together and then disappearing into the woods to search for special springs, whose water was believed to become magical on midsummer's night and to heal wounds and bring a long life.

In Lithuania, young girls make flower garlands with candles placed on them, and put them into a nearby river or lake. If the garland floats, the young girl is sure to get married. In Latvia, young girls throw wreaths into the branches of oak trees in the hope that it will catch there. Each throw counts as one year, so the number of tries equals the number of years the girl will wait to find a husband.

Everyone goes to the countryside to celebrate with singing and dancing. Plenty of fresh, seasonal produce is eaten, including cucumbers, tomatoes and fresh fish. And, as the festival focuses on family and friends, socializing is a major part, with people visiting their neighbours to share beer and cheese – always remembering that it is important never to arrive or leave empty-handed.

St Martin's Day (Martinmas)

For centuries, Martinmas, on 11 November, in the region called Mardipäev, has been one of the most important and cherished days in the Baltic calendar. It celebrates the end of the farming year and the beginning of the winter period. It also marks the end of the period of All Souls, a time when the souls of the ancestors were worshipped, and this lasted from 1 November to Martinmas. St Martin's Day merges the Christian tradition with pagan worship and respect for the dead – and is the Baltic equivalent of Hallowe'en.

Christmas

In the Baltic regions families gather together on Christmas Eve (called Kucia in Lithuania) to eat a ritual supper made from grains and pulses. The table is laid with a white tablecloth over a layer of

Above A sacred procession in the Pyhtitsa Dormition Convent (the Estonian Orthodox Church of Moscow).

straw. The straw represents the manger where Jesus was born, and the souls of the dead are also said to rest upon straw. Twelve foods are prepared to represent the months of the year and the disciples – and none of the dishes is made from meat.

The meal begins when the stars have appeared in the sky. Traditional foods at the Christmas meal are porridge with poppy seed milk, Christmas biscuits, oatmeal pudding, beetroot (beet) soup with mushrooms, pike and herring, mushroom dishes, apples, nuts and cranberry pudding.

If a family member has died during the year, a place is set for them, and in some traditional homes, a homeless or poor person will be invited to join them.

Left Vilnius girls in traditional dress posing for a photograph during a midsummer national street festival.

Baltic food traditions

What is it about the Baltic States that makes their cuisine unique? These three small countries whose land has been a battleground for so many centuries have managed to preserve their own traditions of food and farming, festivals and celebrations, while happily incorporating the ingredients brought by the invaders as it suits them. The emphasis is on fresh foods, using the local crops and livestock. The diet of the region is simply cooked, and is based around warming, filling fare suited to a land of hungry workers and their growing families.

A rural cuisine

The Baltic cuisine has always been dominated by the agricultural landscape. Food had to be based on what could be grown locally and whatever was available during the severe winters, the mild spring and autumn and the warm, damp summers. In the summer many recipes are based on fish from the many lakes, rivers and streams, or from the Baltic Sea. During the winter, when the fresh water and sometimes the sea can freeze, salted, smoked and marinated fish are eaten, preserved from the summer catches. In the autumn they slaughter their sheep; in winter, the pigs; and in spring, the calves.

Veal and pork are still part of the staple diet. Dairy produce from the cows and sheep, including delicious homemade cheeses and butter, has always been popular, and in the summer and autumn everyone picks wonderful varieties of berries and mushrooms, and farmers harvest their fields of grain.

The Balts are fortunate in the quality of ingredients that are available to them, and are now free to revel in a tradition of local cuisine that is robust and rustic, using the freshest and most natural ingredients during the summer and preserving those same ingredients according to time-honoured recipes during the winter.

Daily diet in the Baltic States

There may be slight variations between the countries in daily diet and the regional ingredients, but the pattern is the same for most Balts. On an average day people usually eat a moderate breakfast before going to work. Breakfast will usually be based on rye bread, with cheese, sausage, eggs, tomatoes or cucumber, washed down with coffee or tea (usually black). For many Latvians the day is not imaginable without a drink of milk, usually taken at breakfast time.

All three countries still consider lunch to be the main meal, eaten between midday and 3 p.m. It will consist of something cooked, often some kind of meat (pork chops, rissoles, sautéed fillet, steak, chicken) or fish (salmon, trout, cod, herring, pilchards), with potatoes, boiled rice or buckwheat, and a fresh salad. Sour cream or a cream-based sauce is usually eaten as an accompaniment. Some people also eat soup as a main dish, usually made with meat or fish stock, plus onions, carrots and other vegetables such as

Far left Pumpkins displayed at a farmer's market in Riga, Latvia.
Left Harvesting in Lettland, Latvia, of the beet crop Mangelwurzel. Traditionally used as a stock feed, the roots and leaves are also eaten, lightly steamed or boiled.

Above A butcher preparing his wares in a shop in Vilnius, Lithuania.

Right Customers at this bakery and café in Riga can choose from freshly prepared baguettes, potato and corn breads, as well as cakes and sweet pastries.

potatoes, beetroot (beet), sauerkraut, beans, peas, sorrel or even fresh nettles. The Balts really love their sweet desserts, and there are many different kinds, usually made of dairy products and fruit. The drink to accompany lunch is often one of the delicious fruit juices based on berries or orchard fruit, kefirs (cultured milk), fresh milk, tea or coffee.

Supper is served at around 6 or 7 p.m. This meal is a matter of family preference – it can consist of soup, mixed salads, or a hot meal similar to lunch. Sometimes a more traditional food will be eaten, such as a milk-based soup. Many people now buy ready-made or frozen foods, or simply eat sandwiches or rolls with a cup of tea. Latvians also have a taste for pastries and other bakery products.

Entertaining

"If you do not love other people, you will not be loved" is a translation of a Lithuanian saying. It illustrates how the Balts have always felt about entertaining. When guests are expected, no time or expense will be spared to make them feel welcome. The emphasis is on the friendly sharing of food, sitting round the table with the family, passing and sharing drinks, with plenty of toasts for good health. Beer and mead, the two staples of Baltic drinking, are still popular today, both at home and in restaurants and cafés.

It doesn't take much to encourage an Estonian, Latvian or Lithuanian to burst into song. Singing accompanies every celebration and there are traditional songs about beer, barley and grain, all sung in praise of the host's food and drink.

When guests leave, they are often presented with a small parting gift of food. A particularly honoured guest will be accompanied to the door, where one last drink will be shared with the host.

Left Traditional mealtime festivities at a birthday party in Lithuania.

The influence of other countries

First Germany, then Sweden and Denmark, and finally the USSR have left their imprint on the food traditions of the Baltic States. This has sometimes been an unhappy experience of alien food being forced on an unwilling population; however, some recipes, ingredients and traditions have been adopted enthusiastically by the people of these three countries, especially those based on the vegetables brought from farther afield in the 18th century. The Lithuanians, in particular, have many recipes based on the humble potato, which is transformed into dumplings, pancakes, soups or main dishes, or simply fried as an accompaniment to meat and salad.

Germany added much to the cuisine of the Baltic States, especially in Estonia, where sweet loaves are baked in the German style for special feasts, plaited into unusual shapes and sprinkled with dried fruit and nuts. Because the population of past centuries would have relied on their local produce, the more elaborate German recipes were seen as new and exciting.

The USSR had the greatest influence on the cooking of the Baltic States during the 20th century. Extraordinary as it may seem now, local recipes were suppressed by the Soviets for being 'nationalistic'. An 'Estonian' cookbook produced in 1955 had just 18 pages of Estonian recipes at the back of a publication of more than 400 pages. As a result of this, traditional foods fell out of favour and older methods of cooking began to be forgotten. Recipes such as beetroot (beet) and potato salads, pierogi (dumplings) and Baltic herring dishes were mainly preserved by the people who had emigrated to other countries during this century of violent upheaval.

It is hardly surprising that once the Balts were allowed their independence, they looked to see what was new in the food of other countries. Their own cuisine had been pushed aside, and Russian foods and styles had predominated; now the mistrust of their former masters made the people, above all the young, look to the west. They were eager for foreign goods, things that they had never seen or tasted: German sweetmeats, American burgers and ice cream.

Recent years have seen a massive rediscovery and revival of Baltic traditions in food and farming throughout all three countries. So while cultural influences have been diverse, the cuisine still maintains a distinct national character.

Below Pierogi are the Polish version of filled dumplings. Traditional pierogi fillings use sauerkraut, potato or cabbage.

Below Borscht beetroot soup has variations throughout Russia, Poland and the three Baltic States.

Below A cook wearing traditional dress grills and serves up sausages for tourists in Riga, Latvia.

Above Lithuanian women dressed in folk costume prepare a traditional dish in the city of Vilnius.

Above Restaurant Alpenrose in Riga, Latvia. Many of the country's top chefs are based in various restaurants around the city.

Regional specialities

Each of the three countries of the Baltic States has its own signature dishes. The local climate has a lot to do with how these have evolved, with Lithuania in the milder south capable of growing much more tender crops and raising different kinds of meat and vegetables than the bleaker, colder northern country of Estonia.

Estonian food is based principally on a peasant diet. The inhabitants of this chilly country had to devise all sorts of ways to preserve meat, fish and vegetables for use during the winter months; hence the emphasis on wonderfully fresh food during the summer, and pickled vegetables such as sauerkraut, pork sausage and smoked fish during the winter. The famous Baltic dish, sült, is a regional

favourite – a jellied concoction featuring all the parts of a pig that might otherwise be wasted, including the ears and trotters. Dairy products are popular, especially yogurt, fermented milk and curd cheese.

In Latvia, with its long coastline and its harbour capital in the Gulf of Riga, fish dishes are important all the year round. Meat is still a vital part of the diet, especially pork in all its forms, such as ham and sausage, as well as fresh chops and cutlets. The food is generally fairly bland, with an emphasis on good quality ingredients rather than spices and herbs.

In Lithuania, the warmer climate encourages fresher, lighter recipes such as cold soup, which is very refreshing in the summer. Salads and vegetables are plentiful and the potato is very popular.

It forms the basis of many savoury and sweet recipes such as potato and apple baba, or potato pancakes served with honey and curd cheese.

Bread and beer

The thread that joins all three Baltic countries is their consumption of rye bread and beer. Rye bread is an incredibly basic, staple food in Lithuania, Latvia and Estonia, with all sorts of traditions associated with it. It is eaten at every meal and between meals for a snack. In Lithuania, rye bread is always referred to as female, and if a piece should fall to the ground, tradition dictates that it should be picked up and kissed before being eaten.

Beer is brewed in all parts of the Baltic, and varies in colour from a dark malt, barley or rye beer to a lighter beer. The local brewers keep many traditional recipes going and beer is still by far the most popular drink, whether it is taken on its own or with a meal.

Classic Baltic ingredients

The wildly contrasting seasons of extremely cold winters and hot summers in the Baltic States is reflected in their choice of food throughout the year. Hearty meals for the winter months often include meat dishes and substantial soups. In summer, though, more fish will be eaten and, as there is a glut of berries, the filling winter soups are replaced by light, summer berry soups. When the mushroom season arrives, people living in the eastern areas have fabulous wild mushrooms to add richness to their dishes.

Fish and shellfish
The Baltic States have plentiful supplies of fish from the sea and from the lakes and rivers, so this healthy food is a staple in the region. The Latvians, in particular, share a love of fish, and the markets of Riga are filled with every variety available. Perch, roach, pike, ruff and carp are just some of more than 25 species of freshwater fish that are eaten throughout the Baltic States; sea fish include sprats, eel, cod, haddock, salmon, sardines, halibut and sole and, of course, herring – the favourite.

The Baltic herring is smaller than its Atlantic cousin and is considered to have leaner meat. It can be bought in many states: fresh, frozen, salted, smoked, pickled, raw, fermented and canned. Although not quite as affordable as it has been in the past,

due to overfishing and pollution in the Baltic Sea, it remains the most important fish in the Baltic economies.

Cured fish such as smoked eels and gravlax, which is a salmon cured with flavourings such as dill and peppercorns, are also enjoyed.

Meat and poultry
Pork has always been the most widely eaten meat in the Baltic region, and pigs are often kept by families for slaughtering in December or January to provide fresh pork for the winter – the time when meat dishes tend to be the most popular. Prime cuts of pork and beef will be roasted, but there are also many recipes using minced (ground) meat: as stuffings for cabbage leaves or pastries, or to make meat loaves or patties. Lamb and veal are also eaten,

particularly in the spring, and now that poultry has become more affordable there are several dishes using that, too. Chicken breast fillets will be stuffed with wild mushrooms and rolled. For Christmas, the traditional Lithuanian dish of roast goose is still the first choice and it will be stuffed with sauerkraut, apples, prunes and smoked pork sausage.

Herbs and flavourings
The most widely used herb in the Baltic States is the aniseed-flavoured dill, and this is often grown throughout the region in yards or indoors in pots convenient for picking. The flavour goes well with cool summer soups, and it is added to sour cream in pancakes, to

Below, left to right: Herring; smoked bacon; and wild elderberries.

Above, left to right Wild mushrooms; wild berries including raspberries, blueberries, blackberries and red and white currants; and poppy seeds.

mash and sauerkraut, and to fish. Both the seeds and its attractive foliage are used, although sparingly, as the strong flavour can easily overwhelm other flavours in a dish; the leaves must be added at the end of cooking to preserve their flavour.

The distinctive taste of the caraway seed is much loved by the Baltic population and it appears in a surprisingly vast number of recipes, both savoury and sweet. The seeds are added to baked foods, dumplings, cream cheese and meat dishes, and may also be toasted beforehand to bring out the flavour.

Poppy seeds are also a favourite addition to cakes and breads, giving them a deliciously nutty crunch. They can be roasted or crushed before using to maximize their taste to the full.

Also ubiquitous in Baltic cuisine is the juniper berry, another ingredient used for its distinctive fruity kick that combines so well with savoury dishes. Other flavourings include the fiery tones of mustard and of horseradish.

Foods from the wild

The Balts have always found many superb foods in the wild, particularly honey, mushrooms and berries.

In the summer there is a vast selection of berries for picking. These include wild strawberries, blueberries, cloudberries, blackberries, bilberries, raspberries, loganberries, elderberries and cranberries, as well as red and white currants. The Balts are good at making a thick berry custard, and kissel, as well as compôtes, and a combination of berries and rhubarb are particular favourites. Cranberries are cooked in savoury dishes, whereas the sweet berries are made into preserves or used as toppings for cheesecakes – or simply eaten on their own.

Summers in the Baltic States are generally cool and rainy – perfect for mushrooms. The season starts in the middle of July, and the mushrooms are so abundant that the pickers can select the youngest and choicest specimens. Among almost 4,000 species of fungi in the region about 70 are edible and most are found in the perfect growing conditions of the vast forest floors. Wild mushrooms grow more prolifically in the eastern parts of the countries and so are more commonly eaten there.

Poppy seed milk

This traditional smoothie, which has no dairy element, is used to celebrate the first day of winter.

1 Put 250g/9oz poppy seeds into a bowl, add 750ml/1¼ pints/3 cups boiling water and leave for 10 minutes.

2 Transfer the water and seeds to a blender and whizz for 3–4 minutes, or until completely smooth.

3 Leave to cool, then filter through muslin (cheesecloth). Discard the pulp and return the liquid to the blender.

4 Whizz again, filter once more, then add 30ml/2 tbsp sugar and 5ml/1 tsp almond extract. Chill, and use for making milk smoothies.

Above, left to right Sour cream is used with both savoury and sweet dishes; beetroot features frequently; and ground almonds are used to give extra flavour to desserts.

Dairy produce

The Balts have always enjoyed dairy products. Milk, the milk drink rugaspiens, cottage cheese, cream, cheese and butter are eaten at most meals. Milk is used in many soups, in porridge and for poaching fish. Sour cream is frequently added to recipes, either for pouring over fruit or fruit crumbles, and as a component of prepared meals. Sour cream with dill or honey might accompany fish or meat, be poured over meat dumplings, used when braising meats, or added to a pancake batter or cakes, cheesecakes or in a pastry dough.

Vegetables

Root vegetables make good, hearty additions to meals, and potatoes are served to accompany most meat and poultry dishes. The swede (rutabaga) is also added to soups. Several soups use beetroot (beets), including the Lithuanian version of the famous Russian borscht, and beetroot will also be used in salads, sometimes with herring.

Sauerkraut originally developed as a way to preserve the glut of cabbages, and these continue to be an essential ingredient. This strongly flavoured fermented white cabbage is added to soups and stuffings, combined with mashed potatoes, braised in beer, stuffed in goose or served on its own. Most people make their own sauerkraut, by finely shredding white cabbage and layering it with salt. It is then covered with water and allowed to ferment. Fresh, homemade sauerkraut has a crunchier texture than shop-bought, as well as a delightfully tangy flavour.

Fruit and nuts

Apples are one of the most commonly used fruits, as well as berries and rhubarb, and are added to cakes and desserts as well as used for making compôtes. Prunes and apricots give rich flavours to stuffings for savouries, and fruit is often combined with savoury dishes, as stuffings or cooked alongside them. Candied peels and glacé (candied) fruits such as cherries make the rich, cheese dessert, paskha.

The most frequently used nuts are almonds, added ground to cakes and desserts or flaked (sliced) as toppings.

Grains

The Baltic people make porridges and stews with the tough crops that can withstand the Baltic winters: rye, barley, oats, millet, wheat and buckwheat. Rye remains the most important crop, and the flour is used for the staple food, rye bread. Barley is another much-used grain. It gives bulk and flavour to soups and the flour is also used for bread. Buckwheat flour is made into the traditional blinis (see opposite page). Wheat and oats are the least frequently eaten grains in the region.

Breads, cakes and pastries

Rye bread is the most popular bread and the Balts also produce a variety of soda breads, some with cheese or flavoured with fennel. Pancakes are also enjoyed, and some are made extra light using whisked egg white; and almost all are served with preserves. Leftover bread makes a homely bread pudding flavoured with raisins, apples and cream, which is then served with the ever-popular fruit preserve. Cheesecakes with berry sauces, cakes with fruits, gingerbread and cookies flavoured with caraway or crunchy with poppy seeds are all found in the region.

Above, left to right Rye bread; kvass, a traditional bread drink; and Black Balsams, the national drink of Latvia.

Drinks

As well as tea or coffee, the Balts enjoy fruit juices or spring water, often from natural springs. In Latvia, two of the most popular traditional drinks are ruguspiens (curdled milk that contains no additives) and kefirs (cultured milk). Other beverages include poppy seed milk, a non-alcoholic drink made from yeast, called kvass, and fresh or fermented birch juice and beer. Many people make their own beer at home for the holidays, but there are plenty of commercial breweries: Saku and Tartu in Estonia, and in Latvia, the brewer Aldaris. The most notable Lithuanian beers are Utenos and Kalnapilis.

Vodka made from potatoes was drunk in the Baltic long before the Russians' arrival, but more recently the process uses grains. The thick dark liqueur Riga Black Balsams is drunk with sweet pastries or poured over ice cream, and includes Peruvian balsam oil, arnica blossoms and raspberry juice.

Mead is also a traditional drink, made on the farmsteads from the honey of wild bees, and its quality improves with age.

Blinis

Makes 30–40 (small)

165g/5½oz buckwheat flour

150ml/¼ pint/⅔ cup warm milk

10g/¼oz caster (superfine) sugar

1 tsp salt

2 eggs, separated

10g/¼oz fresh yeast

15ml/1 tbsp sour cream

100g/3¾oz clarified butter

1 Place the flour in a large mixing bowl and make a well in the centre.

2 Warm the milk slightly. Add the sugar and salt and mix well.

3 Stir in the egg yolks and yeast, and mix together until dissolved. Pour into the flour well, and slowly combine until the mixture is smooth. Leave covered in a warm place until the blini dough has doubled in size, for about 1–2 hours.

4 Stir the sour cream into the blini dough. Whisk the egg whites to soft peaks and fold them into the blini dough.

5 To cook, place a heavy non-stick frying pan on a high to medium heat and brush the surface with some butter using a pastry brush.

6 Using a dessert spoon, ladle spoonfuls of the dough, a few at a time, into the frying pan. Cook for about 40 seconds until golden brown, then flip over with a spatula and cook for another 40 seconds.

Soups

Cabbage, nettles, cranberries and sweet rye

Hearty or light, hot or cold – soups play a major role in the dishes of Estonia, Latvia and Lithuania. Unlike Russian cuisine, there are as many cold soups as hot, which may come as a surprise to those from outside the region, who might expect the soups to be heavy and hearty, suitable for the cold winters. But summers in the Baltic tend to be hot, and so cooling soups are popular.

Soups from the region are made from fruits, milk, meat, vegetables and bread, and sweet soups are enjoyed just as much as savoury. Some, such as borscht, have countless variations, and the culinary influences are numerous: from Russia and Poland as well as from the Scandinavian region.

Many of the soups in this chapter are simple ones, based on a peasant tradition. The Lithuanian Pork, Beef and Sauerkraut Soup is a typical example of a soup that makes use of leftover meat, in this case combined with sauerkraut to create a flavoursome, warming dish. Also included are the more sophisticated Chicken Soup with Klimbit Dumplings, the milk- and semolina-based soup Creamy Butternut Squash and Semolina, as well as the fine and delicate Estonian Raspberry Soup for a cool summer dessert.

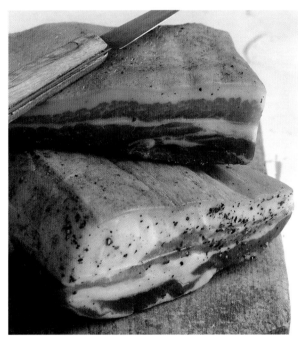

Latvian Barley and Mushroom Soup

Barley and mushrooms are two of the most common ingredients to be found in the Latvian kitchen, and, because Latvians are fond of soups, it is hardly surprising that they combine them in this cold dish.

1 Put the barley in a large bowl and cover with cold water. Soak overnight in a cool place, then drain. Heat the oil in a large, heavy pan and cook the onions for 5 minutes, or until softened but not browned.

2 Add the mushrooms and cook for a further 10 minutes. Add the lemon juice and barley, and stir well. Pour in the stock, then bring to the boil. Simmer for 45 minutes, or until the barley is cooked and soft. Season to taste, then leave to cool.

3 Stir in the sour cream and dill, reserving a little dill to garnish. Chill the soup, then ladle the cold soup into bowls and serve, garnished with the chopped eggs and dill.

Per portion Energy 247kcal/1033kJ; Protein 6.6g; Carbohydrate 23.4g, of which sugars 2.1g; Fat 14.9g, of which saturates 5.3g; Cholesterol 83mg; Calcium 67mg; Fibre 1.3g; Sodium 44mg.

Serves 6

150g/5oz/generous ½ cup pearl barley

45ml/3 tbsp vegetable oil

1 onion, thinly sliced

400g/14oz/5½ cups mushrooms, thinly sliced

45ml/3 tbsp lemon juice

1 litre/1¾ pints/4 cups vegetable stock

200ml/7fl oz/scant 1 cup sour cream

45ml/3 tbsp dill, finely chopped

salt and ground black pepper

2 hard-boiled eggs, finely chopped

Serves 4

450ml/³⁄4 pint/scant 2 cups semi-skimmed (low-fat) milk

1.5ml/¹⁄4 tsp freshly grated nutmeg

250ml/8fl oz/1 cup vegetable stock

400g/14oz butternut squash cut into small cubes

30ml/2 tbsp semolina

salt and ground black pepper

30ml/2 tbsp golden (light corn) syrup, to serve

Cook's Tip When preparing semolina, always stir or whisk the mixture vigorously to keep it smooth and avoid the appearance of lumps.

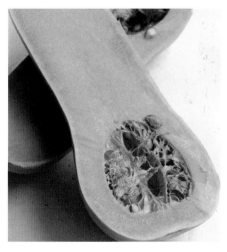

Creamy Butternut Squash and Semolina Soup

Estonians love their soups: cold in the summer months and hot, nourishing and rich during the winter. This soup can be made from all kinds of root vegetables, which are abundant in the late autumn and winter. The use of semolina in soups and puddings is typical of the region. This recipe is often made with swede, but butternut squash also works exceptionally well.

1 Put the milk in a large pan and bring to the boil, then immediately reduce to a simmer. Add the nutmeg and the stock, then season to taste.

2 Add the butternut squash to the simmering milk and stock. Cook until the butternut squash is soft. Adjust the seasoning to taste.

3 Sprinkle with the semolina, stirring constantly to make sure there are no lumps. Cook for 5–6 more minutes, or until the semolina is cooked and the soup has thickened. Ladle into soup bowls and serve drizzled with golden syrup.

Per portion Energy 91kcal/386kJ; Protein 5.2g; Carbohydrate 13.6g, of which sugars 7.3g; Fat 2.3g, of which saturates 1.2g; Cholesterol 7mg; Calcium 165mg; Fibre 1.2g; Sodium 63mg.

Serves 6–8

20g/¾oz/1½ tbsp butter

15ml/1 tbsp caraway seeds

800g/1¾lb beetroot (beets), grated

1 small red cabbage, finely shredded

1 large cooking apple, grated

30ml/2 tbsp vinegar (any kind)

2 carrots, grated

1 bay leaf

2 garlic cloves

2 litres/3½ pints/8¾ cups chicken stock

salt and ground black pepper

3 hard-boiled eggs, chopped, to garnish

100ml/3½fl oz/scant ½ cup sour cream, to serve

Cook's Tip Cooking the mushrooms separately, instead of adding them with the onion, produces a fresher result in the finished soup.

Lithuanian Borscht

Most people think that borscht is a Russian dish, but in fact the original borscht comes from Ukraine. Lithuania also has many different types of this soup, both hot and cold. This version, which contains red cabbage, carrot and apple as well as beetroot, is flavoured with caraway seeds – a Lithuanian favourite – and bay.

1 Heat the butter in a large, heavy pan over a medium heat. When melted, add the caraway seeds and beetroot, and stir to coat in the butter. Season to taste.

2 Add the cabbage and apple to the pan, then the vinegar, carrots, bay leaf and garlic, and pour in the chicken stock. Cover and simmer gently for 2 hours, adding a little water if the liquid reduces too much.

3 Serve the hot borscht topped with the chopped hard-boiled egg, and hand the sour cream round separately.

Per portion Energy 109kcal/456kJ; Protein 5g; Carbohydrate 13.2g, of which sugars 12.4g; Fat 4.4g, of which saturates 2g; Cholesterol 77mg; Calcium 62mg; Fibre 3.8g; Sodium 121mg.

Latvian Nettle Soup

Nettles are loved all over the Baltic region and there are several traditional variations on the theme of nettle soup, some enriched with egg. This Latvian version has a hard-boiled egg topping and is a nutritious and tasty dish to make when nettles are young.

1 Put the nettles in a large bowl and pour over enough boiling water to cover, leave for 30 seconds to blanch, then drain.

2 Heat the butter in a pan over a medium heat, then add the shallot and garlic, and cook for 5 minutes, or until softened but not browned. Sprinkle in the cornflour and stir until smooth, then slowly add the stock, stirring, until smooth. Simmer for 5 minutes, then add the nettles. Continue to cook for 5–6 more minutes. Season to taste.

3 Transfer the nettles and stock to a food processor or blender, and process until smooth. Return to the pan and gently heat through until simmering. Ladle into bowls and add some chopped egg to each. Serve the sour cream separately to add to the soup to taste.

Per portion Energy 62kcal/256kJ; Protein 2.9g; Carbohydrate 3.5g, of which sugars 0.9g; Fat 4.1g, of which saturates 1.9g; Cholesterol 69mg; Calcium 55mg; Fibre 0.7g; Sodium 79mg.

Serves 6

4–5 handfuls of young nettles (see Cook's Tip)

15ml/1 tbsp butter

1 shallot, finely chopped

1 garlic clove, crushed

15ml/1 tbsp cornflour (cornstarch)

500ml/17fl oz/2¼ cups strong chicken stock, heated

salt and ground black pepper

2 large hard-boiled eggs, chopped

100ml/3½ fl oz/scant ½ cup sour cream, to serve

Cook's Tip Nettles are suitable for eating only in spring when they are young and tender and the plants are no more than 20cm/8in high. Use gloves to pick them – you may find rubber gloves are easier than gardening gloves to pick out the tender tops. Wash the nettles well.

Cold Beetroot Soup

This beetroot soup, called chlodnik, is a variation of the famous borscht – always served cold and eaten only in the summer months. There are many versions, but this one has a particular Lithuanian influence in its use of radishes. Because several of the ingredients are raw, the soup is full of vitamins, and it also has a pronounced flavour and vibrant colour.

1 Grate the beetroot (wearing rubber gloves is a good idea) and put into a large bowl. Grate the radishes and cucumber and add to the beetroot.

2 Add the chopped onions. Put a small amount of the vegetable mixture aside. Then pour in the cold stock and yogurt. Combine well, season to taste and chill for at least two hours for all the flavours to unify. Ladle into soup bowls and add the finely chopped dill and the grated vegetables for garnish.

Per portion Energy 89kcal/377kJ; Protein 5.3g; Carbohydrate 16.5g, of which sugars 15.5g; Fat 0.7g, of which saturates 0.2g; Cholesterol 0mg; Calcium 126mg; Fibre 4.1g; Sodium 145mg.

Serves 6

1kg/2¼lb raw beetroot (beets), boiled and peeled

5 bunches pink radishes

2 large cucumbers, peeled

2 bunches spring onions (scallions), finely chopped

1.2 litres/2 pints/5 cups cold chicken or vegetable stock

200ml/7fl oz/scant 1 cup natural (plain) yogurt

salt and ground black pepper

1 large bunch of dill, finely chopped, to garnish

Cook's Tip This soup freezes well. So double the quantities and use individual containers to freeze in portions.

Serves 4

600g/1lb 5oz/3½ cups raspberries

45ml/3 tbsp caster (superfine) sugar

1 cinnamon stick

juice of ½ lemon

30ml/2 tbsp thick natural (plain) yogurt

fresh mint sprigs, to garnish

Estonian Raspberry Soup

Berry picking is much loved by Estonians, and they often use the berries to make preserves, but they are also extremely keen on cold berry soups. Considered a speciality by the restaurants of Tallinn, this soup – malinovyi sup – is traditionally prepared using whichever berries are in season, but raspberries are particularly good.

1 Put the raspberries, sugar and cinnamon stick into a large pan with 500ml/ 17fl oz/2¼ cups water. Add the lemon juice and bring to the boil. Reduce the heat and simmer for 15 minutes, then set aside to cool completely.

2 Transfer the raspberries and liquid to a food processor or blender and process until smooth. Pass through a fine sieve (strainer) and chill until ready to serve. Ladle into soup bowls and spoon a dollop of yogurt on top, then garnish with a sprig of fresh mint and serve.

Per portion Energy 86kcal/370kJ; Protein 2.6g; Carbohydrate 19.2g, of which sugars 19.2g; Fat 0.5g, of which saturates 0.2g; Cholesterol 0mg; Calcium 58mg; Fibre 3.8g; Sodium 12mg.

Cranberry and Apple Soup

Fruit soups are mostly summer dishes, made when fruits and berries are in abundance. This Estonian kissel soup, however, is better suited to later in the year when cranberries are readily available, and it is the perfect accompaniment to festive meals around Christmas and New Year. It has a lovely tart flavour, but if you prefer it sweeter you can add a little more sugar.

1 Put the cranberries in a large pan, cover with water and bring to the boil. Simmer for 10 minutes, or until the cranberries are soft. Allow to cool a little.

2 Transfer the cranberries and liquid to a food processor or blender and pulse to a purée. Pass through a sieve (strainer), pressing down with the back of a spoon to get as much fruit as possible.

3 Discard the fruit pulp and keep the strained fruit and juices. Add the sugar, put back in the pan and gently bring back to a simmer.

4 Add the grated apples to the cranberry mixture. Mix the cornflour with 30ml/ 2 tbsp water to make a smooth paste, then stir into the soup. Simmer, stirring, for 5 minutes. Allow to cool, then transfer to a bowl and chill. Ladle the cold soup into bowls and serve with a dollop of sour cream, swirled with a skewer to decorate.

Per portion Energy 130kcal/552kJ; Protein 1.2g; Carbohydrate 25.1g, of which sugars 22.8g; Fat 3.5g, of which saturates 2.1g; Cholesterol 10mg; Calcium 35mg; Fibre 2.4g; Sodium 12mg.

Serves 6

600g/1lb 5oz/5¼ cups cranberries

200ml/7fl oz/ scant 1 cup water

115g/4oz caster (superfine) sugar

350g/12oz cooking apples, peeled and finely grated

15ml/1 tbsp cornflour (cornstarch)

100ml/3½ fl oz/scant ½ cup sour cream

Serves 6

8 slices of stale rye bread

about 45ml/3 tbsp sugar

1 apple, cored, grated, but not peeled

115g/4oz/1 cup cranberries

115g/4oz/³⁄₄ cup raisins

150ml/¹⁄₄ pint/²⁄₃ cup cranberry juice

1.5ml/¹⁄₄ tsp ground cinnamon

1.5ml/¹⁄₄ tsp ground cloves

grated rind and juice of 1 orange

sour cream, to serve

Cook's Tip If you like, you can chill the soup overnight to eat cold the following day – it will have thickened and tastes good this way.

Estonian Sweet Rye Soup

This bread soup is a typical Estonian dish. There are many variations of soups made with bread throughout Eastern Europe, but this one is distinctive for its sweetness, and the use of rye bread, which is a regional favourite.

1 Put the bread in a large bowl and add 800ml/27fl oz/scant 3¹⁄₄ cups water. Soak for 5 minutes to soften and then transfer to a pan over a medium heat. Add the sugar and simmer for 5 minutes, or until soft.

2 Transfer the mixture to a food processor or blender and pulse until smooth but not puréed. Put back into the pan and add the grated apple, cranberries, raisins and cranberry juice. Mix well to combine and add the cinnamon and cloves.

3 Bring back to the boil, then simmer for 10 minutes. Add the orange juice and rind, taste and add a little more sugar if necessary.

4 Ladle into bowls and serve topped with a dollop of sour cream.

Per portion Energy 167kcal/712kJ; Protein 3.4g; Carbohydrate 39.5g, of which sugars 24.8g; Fat 0.7g, of which saturates 0.1g; Cholesterol 0mg; Calcium 43mg; Fibre 2.4g; Sodium 206mg.

Chicken Soup with Klimbit Dumplings

This is a very popular soup that is much loved in Estonia. The little dumplings are called klimbit and are light and fluffy. They can be added to any type of soup. This is a traditional dish and every Estonian household has their own version. Just about any vegetable benefits from chicken soup's rich flavour, so adapt the recipe around your own favourites.

1 To make the dumplings, first grind the caraway seeds using a mortar and pestle. Sift the flour into a large bowl and add the caraway, sugar and salt. Stir well to mix.

2 In a separate bowl, mix the butter and egg together using an electric whisk, then add the milk. Mix well to combine.

3 Gradually stir the egg mixture into the dry ingredients, mixing well to make a dough. Cover and allow to rest while you prepare the soup.

4 Put the chicken stock in a large pan, bring it to the boil and then reduce the heat. Add the carrots and swede, and simmer the mixture for approximately 15 minutes, or until soft. Adjust the seasoning. Add the peas and chicken meat and return to a simmer.

5 Using a tablespoon, take out spoonfuls of the dumpling dough and drop it into the simmering soup. Add as many as you like – five per serving is about right. Cook until the dumplings have risen to the top of the soup.

6 Sprinkle the soup with the parsley and ladle into soup bowls.

Serves 6

1.2 litres/2 pints/5 cups chicken stock

2 carrots, finely diced

200g/7oz swede (rutabaga), finely cubed

115g/4oz/1 cup peas

300g/11oz boiled chicken meat, shredded

salt and ground black pepper

30ml/2 tbsp fresh parsley, chopped finely, to garnish

For the dumplings

1.5ml/¼ tsp caraway seeds

250g/9oz/generous 2 cups plain (all-purpose) flour

1.5ml/¼ tsp sugar

1.5ml/¼ tsp salt

45ml/3 tbsp butter, softened

1 large egg, beaten

175ml/6fl oz/¾ cup milk

Cook's Tip Toast the caraway seeds in a dry pan over a moderately high heat before grinding them – this will release more flavour.

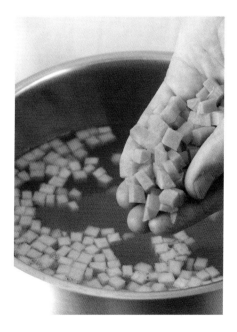

Per portion Energy 317kcal/1332kJ; Protein 18.6g; Carbohydrate 40.3g, of which sugars 6.6g; Fat 10.2g, of which saturates 5.3g; Cholesterol 72mg; Calcium 134mg; Fibre 3.6g; Sodium 135mg.

Lithuanian Pork, Beef and Sauerkraut Soup

This is a one-pot dish that is rich, nourishing and delicious. In Lithuania this soup is made with leftover pork and sauerkraut, but it works superbly well using pork ribs cooked until the meat falls off the bone. You can add any other meat you have, as well as some smoked sausage for added flavour. Use homemade sauerkraut for the most satisfying results. The rich and smoky beef flavour makes this dish the perfect recipe for meat-lovers.

1 Heat 45ml/3 tbsp oil in a large pan over a high heat. Add the caraway seeds, spare ribs, beef and pork. Stir well and brown all over for 6–7 minutes. Season to taste with salt and pepper.

2 Pour in the stock, then reduce the heat to low and simmer for 2 hours, or until the meat is tender. Keep checking the level of the liquid and top up the pan with water if necessary.

3 Meanwhile, put the remaining oil in large, heavy pan and add the bacon and sausage. Sauté for 3 minutes, then add the sauerkraut and paprika. Stir and season with a little salt and pepper. Cook, stirring occasionally, for 20 minutes, or until the sausage is cooked through.

4 Remove the spare ribs with a slotted spoon, and discard the bones, then shred the meat, being careful not to burn your fingers, and return it to the soup pan.

5 Add the sauerkraut and bacon mixture to the pan and mix well. Season to taste and heat gently for another 5 minutes. Serve hot with rye bread.

Serves 8

90ml/6 tbsp vegetable oil

15ml/1 tbsp caraway seeds

600g/1lb 5oz pork spare ribs

300g/11oz good-quality stewing beef, cubed

300g/11oz pork shoulder, cubed

900ml/1½ pints/3¾ cups beef stock

115g/4oz smoked bacon, cubed

400g/14oz smoked pork sausage or kielbasa, cubed

1kg/2¼lb sauerkraut

7.5ml/1½ tsp sweet paprika

salt and ground black pepper

Cook's Tip Make sure that you rinse the sauerkraut well before use.

Variation For some added heat, use hot paprika instead of sweet paprika.

Per portion Energy 543kcal/2254kJ; Protein 39.9g; Carbohydrate 6.8g, of which sugars 2.1g; Fat 39.7g, of which saturates 12.6g; Cholesterol 126mg; Calcium 98mg; Fibre 3g; Sodium 1436mg.

Appetizers, dumplings and side dishes

Wild Mushroom Caviar

Mushrooms Marinated with Juniper Berries

Lithuanian Potato and Apple Baba
with Crispy Rye Topping

Potato and Swede Croquettes

Lithuanian Dumplings with
Cottage Cheese, Swede and Dill

Decorative Baltic Easter Eggs

Lithuanian Omelette with Hemp Seeds

Estonian Sour Cream and
Dill Pancakes

Estonian Cod Salad with Horseradish
and Dill

Marinated Herring

Herring and Beetroot Salad

Homemade Chicken Liver and
Cranberry Pâté

Zeppelins

Lithuanian Mash with Sauerkraut

Lithuanian Potato and Bacon Bake

Traditional Estonian Beer-braised
Sauerkraut with Black Pudding

Baltic Sour Cream and Caraway
Pirucad with Beef

Zeppelins, caviar and salads

In the cuisines of the Baltic, appetizers are often either associated with elements of the great Russian tradition of zakuski or they have similarities with the Scandinavian smorgasbord table.

Many of the first course dishes found in Estonia, Latvia and Lithuania today are light, and frequently use fish. So you will find that gravlax, marinated herrings, smoked eel and cold fish salads with delicious mustard and horseradish dressings feature in almost every home or restaurant menu, but you will also find wonderful vegetable caviars, too.

Dumplings are a favourite dish on almost everybody's table. The delicious Estonian pirukad-stuffed pastries are part of the traditional kohvilaud. In Latvia, almost every household has its own recipe for piragi, or Latvian dumplings, which are similar to the Lithuanian pirogi, with a variety of different fillings. Dumplings are also a traditional food in Russia and Poland and most of the recipes in the Baltic region reflect their influence. Also included in this chapter are the huge and famous, meat-filled and truly delicious Lithuanian dumplings called Zeppelins.

Salads also play a large role in Baltic cuisine and make the perfect appetizers. These are not leaf-based salads but more substantial salads of vegetables, chopped meat or fish – and they are often served as a main meal, too.

Serves 4

15g/½oz/1 tbsp butter

600g/1lb 5oz wild mushrooms, roughly chopped

3 shallots, finely chopped

3 garlic cloves, crushed

60ml/4 tbsp brandy

45ml/3 tbsp double (heavy) cream

30ml/2 tbsp finely chopped fresh chives

30ml/2 tbsp finely chopped fresh parsley

salt and ground black pepper

Variation Use a small amount of dry mushrooms to give a more intense flavour. Dried mushrooms re-hydrate in boiling water in 10–15 minutes.

Wild Mushroom Caviar

The mushroom season in the Baltic States lasts a lot longer than in other parts of Europe, and mushroom picking has become a national pastime. Different versions of mushroom caviar can be found in any of the three Baltic countries; this one is enriched with brandy and is great for topping blini, but is also perfect served on toast. Any mushrooms will do, but a good selection of wild mushrooms will ensure a wonderfully pronounced flavour.

1 Melt the butter in a heavy, non-stick pan over a medium-high heat and add the mushrooms, stirring for 2–3 minutes, or until they release their juices. Add the shallots and garlic to the mushrooms and continue cooking for 6–8 minutes, or until the liquid evaporates and mushrooms are slightly browned.

2 Add the brandy and season with salt and pepper. Cook for a further 2–3 minutes. Add the cream and remove from the heat almost immediately. Allow to cool a little.

3 Put the mushroom mixture in a food processor or blender and pulse to make a rough purée. Transfer into a bowl and add the chives and parsley, mixing well. Adjust the seasoning and serve on toast or as a blini topping.

Per portion Energy 140kcal/579kJ; Protein 3.6g; Carbohydrate 2.5g, of which sugars 1.8g; Fat 10.1g, of which saturates 5.6g; Cholesterol 23mg; Calcium 49mg; Fibre 2.6g; Sodium 45mg.

Mushrooms Marinated with Juniper Berries

A must at the smorgasbord table, marinated mushrooms also make a tasty snack that you will want to keep going back for. The Balts are very fond of them, and they make useful preserves for eating during the long winter months. Every family has a recipe with its own secret ingredient, but there is no secret to this one – it's juniper berries!

1 Grind the bay leaves, cloves, peppercorns and cinnamon using a mortar and pestle, then transfer to a bowl. Add the juniper berries and mix well.

2 Put 175ml/6fl oz/³⁄₄ cup water into a large pan and add the mushrooms and salt. Add the vinegar and spices, then bring to the boil and simmer, stirring occasionally, for 20 minutes; skim off any foam during cooking. Add the garlic and dill seeds just 2 minutes before the end of cooking. Remove the pan from the heat and put it aside to cool.

3 Carefully spoon the mushroom mixture into a jar, and pour the oil on top to seal. Cover tightly and store in the refrigerator for at least 4 days before eating. Once opened, store in the refrigerator and eat within 3 weeks.

Per portion Energy 55kcal/229kJ; Protein 3.9g; Carbohydrate 1.1g, of which sugars 0.7g; Fat 3.9g, of which saturates 0.5g; Cholesterol 0mg; Calcium 37mg; Fibre 2.8g; Sodium 14mg.

Serves 4

2 bay leaves

3 whole cloves

4 black peppercorns

1 cinnamon stick

5 juniper berries, gently crushed

800g/1³⁄₄lb/9¹⁄₃ cups fresh button (white) or small field (portabello) mushrooms

120ml/4fl oz/¹⁄₂ cup white wine vinegar

8 garlic cloves, peeled

2.5ml/¹⁄₂ tsp dill seeds

15ml/1 tbsp vegetable oil

Variation The dill seeds could be substituted with fresh thyme or oregano for a more savoury flavour.

Lithuanian Potato and Apple Baba with Crispy Rye Topping

Apples are a common ingredient in Lithuanian cuisine, used in everything from appetizers to desserts, and rye is the favourite of all the breads, so both ingredients are readily available to make this sweet and fruity side dish. It is the perfect accompaniment to pork, duck or goose.

1 Preheat the oven to 180°C/350°F/Gas 4. Cook the potatoes in a pan of boiling water until tender. Drain and mash with 45ml/3 tbsp milk until smooth and creamy. Keep warm.

2 Melt 15g/½oz/1 tbsp butter in a large shallow frying pan over a medium-high heat and add the apples and sultanas. Cook, stirring constantly, for 5 minutes, then add the nutmeg and honey. Transfer the apple and sultana mixture into the pan with the potatoes and mix well, then add the cream and stir to combine. Season with salt and pepper.

3 Spoon the mixture into an ovenproof dish and sprinkle the breadcrumbs over the top. Melt the remaining butter in a pan and drizzle over the breadcrumbs. Bake for 25 minutes, or until the crumbs have become crisp and golden.

Per portion Energy 225kcal/956kJ; Protein 4.8g; Carbohydrate 43g, of which sugars 15g; Fat 5.2g, of which saturates 2.8g; Cholesterol 12mg; Calcium 60mg; Fibre 2.3g; Sodium 235mg.

Serves 8

500g/1¼lb floury potatoes, peeled and cut into chunks

75ml/2½fl oz/⅓ cup milk, plus 45ml/3 tbsp

25g/1oz/2 tbsp butter

500g/1¼lb green eating apples, peeled, cored and thinly sliced

50g/2oz sultanas (golden raisins)

1.5ml/¼ tsp freshly grated nutmeg

30ml/2 tbsp honey

25ml/1½ tbsp double (heavy) cream

200g/7oz/3½ cups fresh fine rye breadcrumbs

salt and ground black pepper

Variation If you can't find rye bread, use any brown or wholemeal (wholewheat) bread that you have.

Serves 4

2 large baking potatoes, about 500g/1¼lb total weight

250g/9oz swede (rutabaga), diced

25g/1oz/2 tbsp butter

1 large onion, thinly sliced

45ml/3 tbsp plain (all-purpose) flour

75ml/5 tbsp crispy toasted breadcrumbs

2 eggs, beaten

60–90ml/4–6 tbsp rapeseed (canola) oil

salt and ground black pepper

Variations

• If you can't find swede (rutabaga), turnip is a good substitute.

• Use Japanese panko breadcrumbs, to make the croquettes crispier.

Potato and Swede Croquettes

Kaalikas is a type of swede with an attractive yellowish flesh and smooth, creamy texture when cooked. These croquettes are a good alternative to a potato mash – use to accompany roast meat or serve with a salad.

1 Preheat the oven to 200°C/400°F/Gas 6. Bake the potatoes for 1–1½ hours. While the potatoes are cooking put the diced swede into a pan, cover with water and bring to the boil. Reduce the heat and simmer for 15 minutes or until soft.

2 Halve the baked potatoes, and scoop out the flesh into a bowl. Mash to a purée and season. Drain and mash the swede to a purée. Add to the potato and combine.

3 Heat the butter in a frying pan over a medium heat and add the onion. Cook for 8 minutes until softened and lightly golden. Cool slightly and add to the mashed vegetables. Stir well to combine. Leave to cool.

4 Shape into cylinders, 7.5cm/3in long and 3cm/1¼in in diameter. Put the flour on a plate, the breadcrumbs on another and the beaten eggs in a bowl. Dip the croquettes in flour, then in the beaten egg. Finally dip in the breadcrumbs to coat.

5 Heat the oil in a frying pan over a medium heat and add the croquettes. Cook until golden brown, turning so that they cook evenly. Serve hot, seasoning to taste.

Per portion Energy 397kcal/1664kJ; Protein 9.2g; Carbohydrate 48.4g, of which sugars 8.1g; Fat 20g, of which saturates 5.5g; Cholesterol 110mg; Calcium 105mg; Fibre 3.9g; Sodium 229mg.

Lithuanian Dumplings with Cottage Cheese, Swede and Dill

There are so many varieties of dumplings from the kitchens of the Baltic States that it is difficult to choose one in particular. These dumplings can be made days ahead, and then boiled or frozen until needed. They are similar to Polish pirogi, a predictable influence as there are established, strong links between Lithuania and Poland.

Serves 6

300g/11oz/scant 3 cups plain (all-purpose) flour, plus extra for dusting

2 eggs

salt and ground black pepper

75g/3oz/6 tbsp butter, melted, to serve

For the filling

300g/11oz swede (rutabaga) or turnips, diced

200g/7oz/scant 1 cup cottage cheese

1 bunch spring onions (scallions), finely chopped

1 bunch fresh dill, finely chopped

Variation If you have any leftover dumplings they are delicious sautéed in a little butter then served with a drizzle of sour cream and a sprinkling of dill.

1 Cook the swede or turnips for the filling in a pan of boiling water until tender. Drain and mash, then set aside to cool.

2 In a food processor mix the flour, eggs, a pinch of salt and 60–75ml/4–5 tbsp water to make a smooth dough. (Alternatively, put the flour and salt in a bowl and stir in the eggs and water using a wooden spoon, then use your hands to make the dough.) Work the dough on a board until it is smooth and elastic.

3 Divide the dough in half and roll each half into a thin sheet on a floured surface. (Use a pasta machine, if you have one.) The dough should be about the thickness of ravioli. Cut the rolled dough into small rounds, 13–15cm/5–6in in diameter, using a pastry (cookie) cutter or a glass.

4 To make the filling, add the cottage cheese to the mashed swede, with the spring onions and dill, reserving a little to garnish. Mix well and season with salt and pepper.

5 Arrange a spoonful of the filling a little in from one edge of each round, and dampen the dough edges with a little water. Fold over and press the edges of the dough together to make a half-circle. Repeat until all the ingredients are used up.

6 Boil a large pan of water, then drop in the dumplings a few at a time. When the dumplings rise to the top, they are cooked. Serve with a little melted butter poured over the top, and garnished with the reserved dill.

Per portion Energy 336kcal/1410kJ; Protein 12.1g; Carbohydrate 42.6g, of which sugars 4.4g; Fat 14.3g, of which saturates 8.2g; Cholesterol 97mg; Calcium 139mg; Fibre 2.8g; Sodium 254mg.

Makes 24

For the golden eggs

12 eggs

the brown peelings of 8 onions

75–90ml/5–6 tbsp vegetable oil

For the purple eggs

12 eggs

500ml/17fl oz/2¼ cups beetroot (beet) juice

75–90ml/5–6 tbsp vegetable oil

Cook's Tip The golden eggs are displayed still in their shells; the purple eggs are peeled to show the dramatic marble effect.

Variation There are other natural dyes that can be used to decorate Easter eggs; these include elderberries for purple, marigold flowers for yellow and tea leaves to create a rose-tan colour.

Decorative Baltic Easter Eggs

Easter is an important festival all over the Baltic region, and egg painting is a must at this time of year. Although commercial egg colours are widely available, colouring eggs using natural colours gives them a more traditional appearance. There are two methods, one using onion skins and one using beetroot juice. The first involves wrapping up the eggs in onions skins before they are cooked to produce a wonderful golden marble effect. Beetroot juice is another natural colouring that you can use for dyeing your eggs once they are hard-boiled.

1 To make the golden eggs, wrap each egg as well as you can in the onion skins, then wrap in kitchen paper and secure with two rubber bands around each egg.

2 Put the eggs in a large pan with cold water and bring to the boil. Boil the eggs for 9 minutes. Have a large bowl filled with cold water ready and, when the eggs are boiled, lift them out with a slotted spoon and drop them gently into the cold water.

3 When completely cold, lift out of the water, unwrap and dry. Polish the shells with a little vegetable oil using kitchen paper, rub it off and buff them. Place the eggs into a large bowl.

4 To make the purple eggs, put the eggs in a pan of cold water and bring to the boil. Boil the eggs for 9 minutes. Lift them out with a slotted spoon and allow to dry. Tap gently all over the shell with a teaspoon, to crack the shell.

5 Put the beetroot juice in a large bowl and gently drop in the cracked eggs. Cover and leave the eggs to soak in the juice for 2–3 hours; the longer you leave them the deeper the colour will be. Lift out the eggs and peel off the shells. The egg whites will have a purple marbled pattern. Arrange the purple eggs on a platter with some spring flowers.

Per portion Energy 53kcal/221kJ; Protein 3.1g; Carbohydrate 0g, of which sugars 0g; Fat 4.6g, of which saturates 1g; Cholesterol 95mg; Calcium 14mg; Fibre 0g; Sodium 35mg.

Lithuanian Omelette with Hemp Seeds

Hemp and flax have traditionally been used as flavourings in Lithuania, and the nutty taste of hemp seeds goes very well with this onion omelette topped with fried onion rings. Serve with a salad as an appetizer or snack.

1 Put 15ml/1 tbsp oil in a medium pan over a medium heat and add the hemp seeds and half the onion slices. Cook for 2–3 minutes, until the seeds are crispy and the onion softened. Add the caraway seeds and remove from the heat. Leave to cool.

2 Transfer the onion mixture to a mortar and use a pestle to grind it to a smooth paste. Crack the eggs into a bowl, and beat in the onion paste. Season with salt and pepper.

3 Put the remaining onion rings in a bowl with a lid and add the flour and seasoning. Seal the bowl and shake to dust the rings. Pour 45ml/3 tbsp oil into a small frying pan and fry the onion rings, a few at a time, until golden and crispy.

4 To make the omelette, add 15ml/1 tbsp oil to a non-stick frying pan over a medium-high heat and, when hot, pour in the egg mixture. As they set around the edges, lift the omelettes up and tilt the pan to let the uncooked egg run underneath. Cook for 2–3 minutes on each side. Serve, topped with crispy onion rings.

Per portion Energy 654kcal/2713kJ; Protein 24.5g; Carbohydrate 35.6g, of which sugars 14.6g; Fat 47.3g, of which saturates 7.2g; Cholesterol 476mg; Calcium 180mg; Fibre 5.3g; Sodium 184mg.

Serves 2

75ml/2½fl oz/⅓ cup vegetable oil

45ml/3 tbsp hemp seeds

2 large onions, thinly sliced

2.5ml/½ tsp caraway seeds

4 large eggs

30ml/2 tbsp plain (all-purpose) flour

salt and ground black pepper

Makes 20–30

165g/5$\frac{1}{2}$oz wholemeal
(whole-wheat) flour

150ml/$\frac{1}{4}$ pint/$\frac{2}{3}$ cup barely warm milk

10g/$\frac{1}{4}$oz caster (superfine) sugar

5ml/1 tsp salt

2 eggs, separated

10g/$\frac{1}{4}$oz fresh yeast

15ml/1 tbsp sour cream

30ml/2 tbsp finely chopped fresh dill

115g/4oz clarified butter, melted

To serve

100ml/3$\frac{1}{2}$fl oz/scant $\frac{1}{2}$ cup sour cream

150g/5oz gravlax, sliced into strips

fresh dill sprigs

Estonian Sour Cream and Dill Pancakes

Fluffy, melting in the mouth, delicate little pancakes, these were introduced to the kitchens of Estonia by the Russians. They are yeast-raised pancakes, not that dissimilar to Russian blinis.

1 Sift the flour into a bowl, add the bran left in the sieve (strainer), and make a well.

2 Pour the barely warm milk into a separate bowl, add the sugar and salt, and mix well until dissolved. Add the egg yolks and yeast to the milk, and stir to combine.

3 Pour the mixture into the flour well, and slowly stir the flour into the liquid, starting at the centre, until everything is amalgamated and smooth. Cover and leave in a warm place for 1–2 hours, or until the pancake dough has doubled in size.

4 Stir the sour cream into the dough and add the dill. Put the egg whites into a clean, grease-free bowl and whisk until the mixture forms soft peaks. Fold into the pancake dough.

5 Heat a heavy, non-stick frying pan over a medium-high heat and, using a pastry brush, brush the surface with a little butter. Spoon small amounts of the pancake dough and cook gently for about 40 seconds on each side, then remove and keep warm. Serve topped with sour cream, gravlax and dill.

Per portion Energy 31kcal/131kJ; Protein 1.3g; Carbohydrate 4.1g, of which sugars 0.7g; Fat 1.2g, of which saturates 0.5g; Cholesterol 13mg; Calcium 11mg; Fibre 0.5g; Sodium 8mg.

Estonian Cod Salad with Horseradish and Dill

Fish is a frequent component of salads from the Baltic region. Poaching, rather than frying fish, is most typical. When served with a light horseradish and dill sauce, this dish tastes marvellous.

1 Put the cod in a large frying pan and just cover with water. Bring to the boil and simmer for 4 minutes, or until cooked through. Test with a point of a knife; the flesh should flake easily and be milky white. Lift out of the pan, drain and put on a plate.

2 When the fish is cool enough to handle, remove and discard the skin. Gently break the fish into chunky flakes and drizzle with lemon juice.

3 To make the dressing, put the horseradish in a bowl and stir in the sour cream, mayonnaise, onions and dill. Season with salt and pepper.

4 In a large bowl, gently combine the fish, cucumber, watercress or rocket and the dressing. Serve immediately while the fish is juicy and the salad leaves are crunchy.

Per portion Energy 239kcal/997kJ; Protein 33.7g; Carbohydrate 2.1g, of which sugars 2.1g; Fat 10.6g, of which saturates 4.5g; Cholesterol 98mg; Calcium 137mg; Fibre 1.1g; Sodium 159mg.

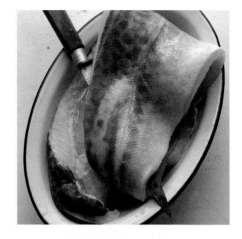

Serves 4

675g/1½lb cod fillets

30ml/2 tbsp lemon juice

1 cucumber, thinly sliced

200g/7oz watercress or rocket (arugula)

For the dressing

10ml/2 tsp creamed horseradish

120ml/4fl oz/½ cup sour cream

15ml/1 tbsp mayonnaise

4 spring onions (scallions), finely chopped

small bunch of dill, finely chopped

salt and ground black pepper

Variation Most fish can be used in place of the cod, with herrings or smoked haddock particular favourites.

Serves 8

8 salted herring fillets

8 peppercorns, crushed

7.5ml/1½ tsp fennel seeds, crushed

7.5ml/1½ tsp juniper berries, lightly crushed

1 red onion, finely sliced

200ml/7fl oz/scant 1 cup white wine vinegar

115g/4oz/⅔ cup caster (superfine) sugar

Cook's Tip Cut the marinated herring into small pieces and serve with warm blinis and sour cream.

Marinated Herring

In the Baltic they say there as many recipes for marinated herring as there are trees in the woods. This is a particular favourite flavoured with the warm tastes of fennel and juniper. It is perfect chopped in salads, as a topping on a blini, as a filling for a sandwich, or simply as a quick snack.

1 You need to remove as much salt from the herrings as possible. To do this, put them in a colander and run them under cold running water for 2 minutes, then put them into a bowl. Cover with cold water and leave to soak for 4 hours. Drain in a colander and rinse thoroughly again.

2 Mix together the peppercorns, fennel seeds and juniper berries in a small bowl. Pat dry the herring fillets with kitchen paper and then layer them in a dish that you can cover or a jar with a lid, alternating the layers with sliced red onion and a sprinkling of the peppercorn mixture.

3 Pour the white wine vinegar into a jug (pitcher) and add 200ml/7fl oz/scant 1 cup water and the sugar. Stir well, then pour over the layered fish, onion and spices.

4 Close the jar or cover the dish and allow to marinate for a few days before using. Eat within 10 days.

Per portion Energy 129kcal/544kJ; Protein 8.4g; Carbohydrate 11.5g, of which sugars 11.5g; Fat 5.6g, of which saturates 0g; Cholesterol 21mg; Calcium 10mg; Fibre 0g; Sodium 415mg.

Herring and Beetroot Salad

Marinated herring goes particularly well with the earthy taste of beetroot and the sweetness of apple in this quick salad. A creamy horseradish dressing makes the dish into the perfect appetizer.

1 Put the diced beetroot into a large bowl. Chop the herring fillets, removing all the bones, and add them to the beetroot. Add the apple and spring onions.

2 To make the dressing, put the creamed horseradish in a small bowl and mix in the sour cream and dill. Season with salt and pepper.

3 Pour the horseradish mixture over the beetroot and herrings, then mix everything gently to combine.

4 Arrange a pile of the beetroot leaves in the middle of each plate and spoon over the herring and beetroot salad, and garnish each with a sprig of dill.

Per portion Energy 222kcal/935kJ; Protein 13.6g; Carbohydrate 21.8g, of which sugars 20.6g; Fat 9.3g, of which saturates 2g; Cholesterol 30mg; Calcium 153mg; Fibre 5g; Sodium 620mg.

Serves 4

3 medium boiled beetroots (beets), finely diced

4 marinated herring fillets

1 apple, sliced thinly into sticks

4 spring onions (scallions), thinly sliced

200g/7oz baby beetroot (beet) leaves

sprigs of dill, to garnish

For the dressing

5ml/1 tsp creamed horseradish

60ml/4 tbsp sour cream

15ml/1 tbsp finely chopped fresh dill

salt and ground black pepper

5ml/1 tsp vegetable oil

2 shallots, finely sliced

500g/1¼lb chicken livers

250ml/8fl oz/1 cup chicken stock

115g/4oz/1 cup cranberries

30ml/2 tbsp Madeira

225g/8oz/1 cup butter, softened

2.5ml/½ tsp ground allspice

90g (3½oz) unsalted butter, cubed

salt and ground black pepper

Homemade Chicken Liver and Cranberry Pâté

Pâtés are very common in the Baltic region, as they are a tasty way of using every part of an animal. Chicken pâté is simple and rich in flavour. Here is a modern version, which includes some zesty cranberries. Serve with crusty rye bread.

1 Put the oil in a deep frying pan and heat over a medium heat. Add the shallots and cook for 2–3 minutes, or until beginning to soften.

2 Add the chicken livers and the stock, and bring to the boil. Reduce the temperature and simmer for 20 minutes, or until the livers are tender.

3 Spoon about 120ml/4fl oz/½ cup of the cooking liquid into a small pan and add the cranberries. Simmer for 3–5 minutes, or until the cranberries are just soft. Drain.

4 Drain the livers, reserving the cooking liquid. When cool, transfer to a food processor or blender, add the Madeira and enough cooking liquid to make a smooth, thick pâté.

5 Add the butter and ground allspice, and process to a smooth pâté. Add the cranberries and mix in well with the pâté. Season to taste. Spoon into a ceramic dish and smooth the surface. Melt the unsalted butter over a medium heat and pour over the pâté (this prevents the pâté from discolouring and lengthens keeping time). Once the butter sets, cover with clear film (plastic wrap), and chill before serving.

Per portion Energy 246kcal/1019kJ; Protein 9.8g; Carbohydrate 1.9g, of which sugars 1.5g; Fat 19.9g, of which saturates 13.2g; Cholesterol 242mg; Calcium 11mg; Fibre 0.3g; Sodium 212mg.

Zeppelins

Didzkukuliai, or Zeppelins, are the most famous Lithuanian dumpling, named after the airship balloons built by Ferdinand von Zeppelin. Absolutely delicious as well as filling, they are made from potatoes with a pork and herb filling, served topped with crispy bacon and sour cream. Traditionally they were served to guests, or eaten before heavy physical work, but now they are enjoyed by everyone and appear on all restaurant menus.

1 Cook the large potatoes in a pan of boiling water until soft. Drain and mash.

2 Wrap the grated potatoes in a piece of muslin (cheesecloth) and squeeze out as much water as possible into a bowl. Put the grated potato into a large bowl. Save the potato liquid and allow it to settle, then discard the thin liquid at the top and keep the starch at the bottom. Mix the starch with the squeeze-dried grated potatoes.

3 Stir the boiled potatoes into the grated potatoes, mixing to combine well. Season with salt and pepper.

4 To make the filling, melt the butter in a frying pan over a medium heat and then add the onion. Cook, stirring constantly, for 2 minutes. Add the pork and cook, stirring, for 5–7 minutes, or until the mince is well broken up and sizzling, and no pink remains, then add the marjoram and thyme. Season with salt and pepper and mix well to combine.

5 Scoop up about 30ml/2 tbsp of the potato mixture and flatten it into a large round. Put a generous amount of the filling in the middle and seal it in by folding the edges over to overlap in the centre, then roll it in your hands to make a long cylindrical shape. Repeat with the remaining potato mixture.

6 Bring a large pan of water to the boil and gently drop in the dumplings. Cook for 30 minutes, stirring very gently from time to time. When they are done they will float to the surface. Then, using a slotted spoon, lift out the dumplings from the pan and put on a serving platter; keep warm.

7 When the dumplings are almost cooked, put the bacon cubes in a heavy frying pan and cook them until crisp. Serve the dumplings topped with the crispy bacon and sprinkled with the fresh marjoram. Put the sour cream in a bowl and hand round separately.

Per portion Energy 344kcal/1451kJ; Protein 19.9g; Carbohydrate 48.4g, of which sugars 8.9g; Fat 9.3g, of which saturates 3.6g; Cholesterol 52mg; Calcium 46mg; Fibre 3.9g; Sodium 90mg.

Serves 4

3 large potatoes, peeled and cut into large pieces

1kg/2½lb potatoes, peeled and grated

salt and ground black pepper

For the filling

5ml/1 tsp butter

1 large onion, grated or finely chopped

300g/11oz minced (ground) pork

5ml/1 tsp finely chopped fresh marjoram

5ml/1 tsp finely chopped fresh thyme

To serve

200g/7oz thick bacon rashers (strips), diced

30ml/2 tbsp finely chopped fresh marjoram

200ml/7fl oz/scant 1 cup sour cream

Serves 4

500g/1¼lb potatoes, peeled and diced

10ml/2 tsp butter

800g/1¾lb sauerkraut, drained and finely chopped

5ml/1 tsp caraway seeds

250g/9oz thick bacon rashers (strips), diced

200g/7oz wild mushrooms, chopped

salt and ground black pepper

30ml/2 tbsp finely chopped fresh dill

Variation Sprinkle some crispy smoked bacon on top of the finished dish for more flavour.

Lithuanian Mash with Sauerkraut

This is a family favourite from Lithuania, called kiunke su kopūstais. It is quite similar to the Irish and Scottish potato and cabbage dish, colcannon, and is usually made to accompany various cuts of grilled meat or fish. Sauerkraut is widely available in the shops, but you will always get the best results if you use a homemade variety.

1 Cook the potatoes in a pan of boiling water until tender. Drain, mash and keep warm. Heat the butter in a large, non-stick frying pan over a medium heat and, when melted, add the sauerkraut and sauté over a medium heat. Cook, stirring, for 3–5 minutes. Stir in the caraway seeds, then transfer to a dish and keep warm until needed.

2 Add the bacon to the pan, and cook, stirring, for 2 minutes. Add the mushrooms and continue cooking for 4–5 more minutes. Season to taste.

3 Add the sauerkraut to the mashed potatoes and mix well. Stir in half the bacon and mushroom mixture and mix well, keeping the mixture over the heat. Check the seasoning and add the dill. Serve hot on a large platter, sprinkling the remaining bacon and mushroom mixture over the top.

Per portion Energy 353kcal/1473kJ; Protein 20.7g; Carbohydrate 30g, of which sugars 5.2g; Fat 17.3g, of which saturates 7.2g; Cholesterol 52mg; Calcium 152mg; Fibre 8.3g; Sodium 2903mg.

Lithuanian Potato and Bacon Bake

This is one of the most famous dishes of Lithuania, called kugelis. It is usually made as a hearty dish that is real comfort food. This is a lighter recipe with less fat than the traditional version. Kugelis is served topped with crispy onion rings.

1 Preheat the oven to 200°C/400°F/Gas 6. Wrap the grated potatoes in a piece of muslin (cheesecloth) and squeeze out as much liquid as possible. Discard the liquid. Put the potatoes into a bowl and stir in the beaten eggs, potato flour and baking powder.

2 Cook the diced bacon in a heavy pan over a medium-high heat, stirring constantly, for 3–4 minutes. Add the shallots and cook for a further 3 minutes. Season.

3 Tip the cooked bacon and shallots into the bowl with the grated potatoes and add the ground caraway seeds and dill. Mix well to combine, then adjust the seasoning.

4 Spoon the potato mixture into an ovenproof dish and bake for 35–45 minutes.

5 To make the crispy onion rings, heat the oil in a pan. Put the onion rings in a plastic bag or a bowl with a lid and add the flour. Seal the bag or bowl and shake to dust the rings. Drop them into the hot oil to cook, in batches, until golden and crispy. Lift out using a slotted spoon and drain. Serve the bake topped with the onion rings.

Per portion Energy 211kcal/888kJ; Protein 10.3g; Carbohydrate 26.3g, of which sugars 2.3g; Fat 7.8g, of which saturates 2.7g; Cholesterol 81mg; Calcium 23mg; Fibre 1.6g; Sodium 552mg.

Serves 6

800g/1¾lb potatoes, peeled and grated

2 eggs, beaten

30ml/2 tbsp potato flour

2.5ml/½ tsp baking powder

200g/7oz bacon, diced

2 shallots, finely chopped

2.5ml/½ tsp caraway seeds, ground

30ml/2 tbsp finely chopped fresh dill

salt and ground black pepper

To serve

100ml/3½fl oz/scant ½ cup vegetable oil

1 large onion, sliced into rings

30ml/2 tbsp plain (all-purpose) flour

Serves 8

1kg/2¼lb sauerkraut

20g/¾oz/1½ tbsp butter

7.5ml/1½ tsp caraway seeds

60ml/4 tbsp light muscovado (brown) sugar

500ml/17fl oz/2¼ cups dark beer

30ml/2 tbsp fresh thyme leaves

350g/12oz black pudding (blood sausage), roughly chopped

thyme sprigs, to garnish

Cook's Tips

• You can use the liquid from sauerkraut for a healthy drink.

• A good black pudding will have a heavy chunky texture, often containing barley as well as a wide range of green herbs. They will be available from specialist Eastern European suppliers.

Traditional Estonian Beer-braised Sauerkraut with Black Pudding

It would be impossible to have a cookbook on Baltic cuisine without including one of the most common recipes in Estonia: sauerkraut cooked with beer. There are many versions of this recipe, but this version is particularly good, topped with crunchy black pudding. Buy the best black pudding you can. Sauerkraut is made in homes all across the Baltic, but it is readily available in most supermarkets.

1 Drain the sauerkraut, reserving the liquid if you want to use it for something else (see Cook's Tip).

2 Put half the butter in a large pan over a medium-high heat and add the caraway seeds. Stir the mixture for 1 minute, and then stir in the sauerkraut. Add the sugar.

3 Pour in the beer and add the thyme leaves, then cover the pan and cook gently for 1 hour, or until the cabbage is soft. Season to taste.

4 Meanwhile, put the remaining butter into a small frying pan and add the black pudding. Cook over a medium-high heat for 6–8 minutes, or until crispy.

5 Serve the beer-braised sauerkraut topped with crispy chunks of the black pudding and garnished with thyme sprigs.

Per portion Energy 209kcal/868kJ; Protein 6.1g; Carbohydrate 17.9g, of which sugars 10.7g; Fat 11.5g, of which saturates 5.1g; Cholesterol 36mg; Calcium 124mg; Fibre 2.8g; Sodium 1173mg.

Baltic Sour Cream and Caraway Pirucad with Beef

Pirucad are typical Estonian pastries, and similar versions can also be found in Russia and Poland, although the Polish pirogi are boiled and not baked as here. The pastry in this recipe is enriched with sour cream and caraway seeds, which makes it exceptionally tasty, enclosing a stuffing of beef with dill. The pastries are eaten as snacks or as a lunch, and often served with potatoes.

Makes 12–15

5ml/1 tsp caraway seeds

225g/8oz/2 cups plain (all-purpose) flour

2.5ml/½ tsp salt

2.5ml/½ tsp baking powder

115g/4oz/½ cup butter, chilled and cubed

2 large (US extra large) egg yolks, beaten

120ml/4fl oz/½ cup sour cream

For the filling

60ml/4 tbsp vegetable oil

1 onion, finely chopped

200g/7oz/scant 1 cup minced (ground) beef

1 small bunch fresh dill, finely chopped

2 egg yolks, beaten

salt and ground black pepper

1 Put the caraway seeds in a dry pan over a medium-high heat and toast them for 1 minute, or until they release their aroma. Set aside.

2 To make the filling, heat the oil in a heavy frying pan and cook the onion for 3 minutes, or until softened. Add the minced beef and cook, stirring frequently, for 10 more minutes. Stir in the dill and egg yolks and season with salt and pepper. Cool until ready to use.

3 Put the flour, salt and baking powder into a large bowl. Rub the butter into the flour by hand or using a pastry (cookie) cutter, to resemble fine crumbs. Stir in the beaten egg yolks and sour cream, a little at a time, working it all together to achieve a smooth and elastic dough. Add the caraway seeds. Knead for 2–3 minutes, then wrap in clear film (plastic wrap) and chill for 1 hour.

4 Preheat the oven to 190°C/375°F/Gas 5 and grease a baking sheet. Roll out the dough to about 5mm/¼in thick. Using a pastry cutter or a glass about 7.5cm/3in in diameter, stamp out as many rounds as you can.

5 Brush the edges of the pastry rounds with beaten egg yolk, and put a spoonful of filling in the centre of each round. Press the edges gently together to make a half-circle shape. Repeat with the remaining dough and filling.

6 Put the pastries on the baking sheet, brush the tops with egg yolk, and bake for 25 minutes. Serve.

Per portion Energy 206kcal/858kJ; Protein 5.3g; Carbohydrate 14.1g, of which sugars 2.1g; Fat 14.7g, of which saturates 6.8g; Cholesterol 85mg; Calcium 47mg; Fibre 0.9g; Sodium 76mg.

Fish and shellfish dishes

Croquettes, bakes and fillets

Fresh fish is found in abundance in the Baltic – this is what makes the region's diet so healthy. Alongside potatoes, fish is placed at the heart of the cooking and many regional recipes combine these two staple foods.

Canned and frozen fish were popular during the years of the Soviet era, but since the late 1980s fresh fish is widely available. Fishing has always been a favourite pastime, and species such as perch, roach, pike, ruff and crayfish are often prepared at home. Recipes using smoked and marinated fish include Thyme and Juniper-baked Haddock and Salmon, Potato and Mushroom Bake. There are also less familiar fish dishes eaten in parts of the Baltic – such as smelts, raimed or Tallinn sprotid – and some of the recipes have been adapted for more easily available varieties, such as Cod Tallinn-style and Stuffed Lemon Sole Fillets with Gratin Sauce. Among all the fish, herring is the supreme ruler, and Baltic recipes using this full-flavoured fish include Juniper Berry Marinated Herring with Red Onion and Estonian Herring, Ham and Beetroot Salad.

Some fish species are under threat, so take care to use sustainable sources. Farmed and Atlantic salmon and king crabs fished outside the USA, for example, are in short supply. Other species less dramatically affected but that need protecting are Pacific cod (trawl) and sole, wild clams and Atlantic herring. Sustainable choices are Pacific cod (bottom longline), Atlantic mackerel, farmed rainbow trout, stone crabs and farmed bay scallops. Advice on ecological sources is given within the recipes. Recommendations are available from organizations such as the World Wildlife Fund and the Environmental Defense Fund (see Useful Addresses on page 126).

Serves 4

900g/2lb white fish fillet (smoked or preferably a combination of smoked and unsmoked), bones and skin removed

60ml/4 tbsp white breadcrumbs, plus 75ml/5 tbsp for coating

100ml/3½fl oz/scant ½ cup milk

75–90ml/5–6 tbsp vegetable oil

1 large onion, thinly sliced

2 eggs, beaten

100ml/3½fl oz/scant ½ cup sour cream

15ml/1 tbsp finely chopped fresh marjoram

15ml/1 tbsp creamed horseradish

2 eggs for rolling croquettes

75ml/5 tbsp flour for rolling croquettes

salt and ground black pepper

Baltic Fish Croquettes

The people of the Baltic States love their croquettes. This recipe would use whichever fish is in season, ideally a mixture of smoked and unsmoked. A cold potato salad and gherkins are traditional and tasty accompaniments.

1 Chop the fish as finely as you can – you can pulse it in a food processor, but make sure that you don't purée it. Transfer the fish into a large bowl.

2 Put the breadcrumbs and milk into a small bowl to soak, squeeze the breadcrumbs dry, and discard the excess milk. Add the breadcrumbs to the fish.

3 Heat 15ml/1 tbsp oil in a frying pan over a medium heat and add the onion. Cook for 3–4 minutes, or until soft but not browned. Add to the fish mixture.

4 Add the eggs to the bowl, with the sour cream, marjoram and horseradish. Season and mix together. Shape the mixture into croquettes as shown. Cover in the egg and the flour, coat in the breadcrumbs and chill for 30 minutes.

5 Heat 30–45ml/2–3 tbsp of the remaining oil in a large non-stick frying pan over a medium heat, and add the fish croquettes in batches, cooking evenly on all sides for 10–12 minutes, or until golden brown and crispy. Serve hot.

Per portion Energy 402kcal/1684kJ; Protein 28.1g; Carbohydrate 33.2g, of which sugars 3.3g; Fat 18.3g, of which saturates 3g; Cholesterol 148mg; Calcium 79mg; Fibre 1.8g; Sodium 622mg.

Cod Tallinn-style

This is a simple and easy recipe to use with cod or any other fish that is available. Strips of breadcrumbed fish are quickly fried, then baked with a sour cream, dill, mustard and cheese topping. Simple, quick and full of flavour, it just needs a salad and new potatoes to serve.

1 Preheat the oven to 200°C/400°F/Gas 6. Melt the butter in a large frying pan over a medium heat.

2 Put the flour on a plate and roll the fish strips in it to coat them evenly. Drop the fish into the melted butter. Season to taste and cook for 2–3 minutes, or until lightly golden, turning halfway through. Add the lemon juice.

3 Remove the fish using a slotted spoon, and arrange, skin side down, on an ovenproof dish, alongside each other.

4 Put the sour cream, dill and mustard in a bowl and mix together. Spread on top of the fish strips and sprinkle with the grated cheese. Bake for 6–8 minutes, or until the top is golden brown and the cheese has melted. Serve hot.

Per portion Energy 331kcal/1384kJ; Protein 41.8g; Carbohydrate 9.9g, of which sugars 1.2g; Fat 13.7g, of which saturates 8g; Cholesterol 127mg; Calcium 165mg; Fibre 0.9g; Sodium 296mg.

Serves 4

20g/³⁄₄oz/1¹⁄₂ tbsp butter

45ml/3 tbsp plain (all-purpose) flour

800g/1³⁄₄lb chunky fillet of cod, cut into thick strips

juice of ¹⁄₂ lemon

75ml/2¹⁄₂fl oz/¹⁄₃ cup thick sour cream

30ml/2 tbsp dill, finely chopped

5ml/1 tsp mild wholegrain mustard

50g/2oz/¹⁄₂ cup grated mild Emmenthal cheese

salt and ground black pepper

Variation Avoid using Atlantic cod. Choose Pacific (bottom longline) cod for best sustainability.

Serves 4

4 large lemon sole fillets (or any other white fish fillet), about 200g/7oz each, skinned and bones removed

10g/¼oz/½ tbsp butter

300g/11oz wild mushrooms, finely chopped

5ml/1 tsp finely chopped fresh tarragon

60ml/4 tbsp white wine

60ml/4 tbsp double (heavy) cream

salt and ground black pepper

For the sauce

7.5ml/1½ tsp butter

1 shallot, finely chopped

15ml/1 tbsp cornflour (cornstarch)

200ml/7fl oz/scant 1 cup fish stock

115g/4oz/1¼ cups freshly grated Parmesan cheese

15ml/1 tbsp finely chopped fresh tarragon

Variation Use chestnut or any other mushrooms if wild are not available.

Stuffed Lemon Sole Fillets with Gratin Sauce

These mushroom-stuffed fillets of white fish are a modern take on an old Latvian recipe, using ingredients that are abundant and real favourites in the Baltic region. A light Parmesan and tarragon sauce makes a succulent topping for the stuffed fish. Serve with steamed vegetables or a salad and potatoes.

1 Lay the fish fillets on your work surface, skin side down. Season with salt and pepper. Melt the butter in a medium pan over a medium heat and add the mushrooms. Stir for 4–5 minutes, or until soft, then add the tarragon. Season with salt and pepper.

2 Add the wine and cream, and cook 5–6 more minutes, or until the liquid has evaporated. Remove from the heat and allow to cool.

3 Preheat the oven to 180°C/350°F/Gas 4. Divide the mushroom mixture between the four fillets of fish, spreading it along the fillets. Roll up the fillets, making sure that the mushroom filling remains inside. Secure with cocktail sticks (toothpicks) and arrange in an ovenproof dish just large enough to hold the fish.

4 To make the sauce, melt the butter in a small pan over a medium heat and add the shallot. Sauté for 1–2 minutes, or until softened. Stir in the cornflour, then gradually add the stock, and combine well to make a smooth sauce. Cook over a low heat for 5 minutes, then add the Parmesan and tarragon.

5 Pour the sauce over the stuffed sole fillet and bake for 20–25 minutes, or until golden brown. Remove from the oven and serve.

Per portion Energy 420kcal/1757kJ; Protein 46g; Carbohydrate 5.1g, of which sugars 1.3g; Fat 23.9g, of which saturates 13.2g; Cholesterol 178mg; Calcium 393mg; Fibre 0.2g; Sodium 545mg.

Thyme and Juniper-baked Haddock

Baking fish in sour cream with typical flavourings from the region is a method of cooking often employed in the Baltic. This recipe uses haddock, but it can be adapted to almost any fish. Delicious served hot or cold, and prepared with either a whole fillet of fish or cut into serving pieces, the dish tastes great with potatoes and steamed vegetables.

1 Preheat the oven to 180°C/350°F/Gas 4. Arrange the haddock fillets in an ovenproof dish that is just large enough to hold them in a single layer. Season with salt and pepper.

2 In a bowl, mix together the thyme, juniper berries and sugar, then rub this mixture into the fillets.

3 Stir the sour cream and pour over the fish. Sprinkle with the dill and bake for 20–30 minutes, depending on the thickness of the fillets. The fish is cooked when it flakes easily when separated with the point of a knife. Serve.

Per portion Energy 357kcal/1485kJ; Protein 36.9g; Carbohydrate 4.5g, of which sugars 4.5g; Fat 21.3g, of which saturates 12.7g; Cholesterol 132mg; Calcium 154mg; Fibre 0.6g; Sodium 285mg.

Serves 4

4 thick haddock fillets, about 200g/7oz each, skin on, bones removed

15ml/1 tbsp finely chopped fresh thyme leaves

2.5ml/½ tsp juniper berries, crushed

1.5ml/¼ tsp sugar

400ml/14fl oz/1⅔ cups thick sour cream

30ml/2 tbsp finely chopped fresh dill

salt and ground black pepper

Variation Avoid using trawl haddock, a fishing method that has resulted in overfishing. A more sustainable option is hook-and-line haddock. Good sustainable alternative fish choices are Pacific cod and Pacific halibut.

Serves 4

5ml/1 tsp caraway seeds, lightly toasted

5ml/1 tsp butter

2 leeks, finely sliced lengthways

3–4 thin carrots, finely sliced

1 parsnip, finely sliced lengthways

2 apples, peeled and finely sliced in wedges

250ml/8fl oz/1 cup vegetable stock

4 fillets smoked haddock, 250g/9oz each, bones removed

salt and ground black pepper

30ml/2 tbsp finely chopped fresh parsley, to garnish

Cook's Tip A light horseradish cream is a delicious accompaniment to this dish.

Smoked Haddock with Vegetables and Apple

This light Lithuanian recipe is full of the fresh flavours of sautéed leeks, root vegetables and apples to complement the smoked haddock, which, as in almost all Baltic recipes, is poached. Smoked cod would be also be perfectly suitable instead of the haddock. Serve with rye bread to soak up the lovely juices.

1 Put the caraway seeds in a dry pan over a medium-high heat and toast them for 1 minute, or until they release their aroma. Heat the butter in a deep pan over a medium-high heat and add the leeks, carrots, parsnip and apples. Season to taste and add the caraway seeds. Turn the heat to medium and cook, stirring gently, for 3–5 minutes.

2 Add the stock and reduce the heat to low. Cook for 10–12 more minutes. Add the fish fillets to the stock, making sure that they are covered by the stock and vegetables. Cook for a further 5 minutes.

3 Remove the fish, using a slotted spoon, and arrange in a deep serving plate. Spoon over some of the cooked vegetables and cooking liquid. Sprinkle with the chopped parsley and serve.

Per portion Energy 323kcal/1368kJ; Protein 51.1g; Carbohydrate 21.8g, of which sugars 17.2g; Fat 4.1g, of which saturates 1.2g; Cholesterol 93mg; Calcium 152mg; Fibre 8.3g; Sodium 1947mg.

Juniper Berry Marinated Herring with Red Onion

Herrings marinated in vinegar and lemon juice with the warm hints of caraway, cloves, mustard and juniper have a strong flavour that is complemented by slices of red onion. Served with mayonnaise and rye bread it makes a tasty lunch dish.

1 Cut the herring fillets into pieces, about 3cm/1¼in each. To make the marinade, put the caraway seeds in a dry pan over a medium-high heat and toast them for 1 minute, or until they release their aroma. Put them in a pan with the remaining ingredients and 60ml/4 tbsp water, and bring to the boil for 2 minutes. Cool and leave aside to infuse (steep) for 1 hour.

2 Add the herring fillet pieces to the marinade and cover. Transfer to the refrigerator and chill for 24 hours.

3 When ready to serve, remove the herring and drain. Discard the marinade. Separate the onion slices into rings. Make a little tower on each serving plate by alternating the onion rings with pieces of herring, finishing with an onion ring. Season to taste, and serve with rye bread and mayonnaise.

Per portion Energy 338kcal/1403kJ; Protein 21.5g; Carbohydrate 11.7g, of which sugars 8.7g; Fat 16.9g, of which saturates 6.5g; Cholesterol 84mg; Calcium 61mg; Fibre 0.2g; Sodium 84mg.

Serves 4

4 fresh herring fillets, about 75–115g/3–4oz each

1 red onion, sliced into rings

rye bread and mayonnaise, to serve

For the marinade

1.5ml/¼ tsp caraway seeds

50ml/2fl oz/¼ cup white wine vinegar

45ml/3 tbsp lemon juice

30ml/2 tbsp caster (superfine) sugar

15 juniper berries, crushed

2.5ml/½ tsp mustard seeds, lightly crushed

4 cloves, crushed

4 bay leaves

Variations More sustainable alternatives to Atlantic herring are sardines, sild, sperling, pilchard or brit.

2 fillets of pickled herring, drained and diced

1 large potato, boiled and diced

2 large cooked beetroot (beets), peeled and diced

1 small onion, grated

2 medium tart apples, cored and cut into thin wedges

2 gherkins, chopped

200g/7oz thick piece of ham, diced

2 thinly sliced hard-boiled eggs

salt and ground black pepper

30ml/2 tbsp finely chopped fresh dill, to garnish

For the dressing

100ml/3½fl oz/scant ½ cup sour cream

15ml/1 tbsp vinegar (any kind)

15ml/1 tbsp wholegrain mustard

1 medium beetroot (beet), finely grated

5ml/1 tsp creamed horseradish

Cook's Tip To give this dish a little extra heat, add a small amount of freshly grated horseradish root.

Estonian Herring, Ham and Beetroot Salad

This is a very modern take on an old classic, Estonian rosolje. This dish is an essential on the smorgasbord table and it is a combination of herring, ham, potatoes and beetroot. It is a common item on menus in many restaurants, as it makes a perfect light snack.

1 To make the dressing, put the sour cream in a bowl and add the vinegar, mustard, grated beetroot and horseradish. Season to taste and combine well. Set aside.

2 Put the herring in a large bowl with the potato, beetroot, onion, apples, gherkins and ham. Season and mix together gently.

3 Add the dressing to the mixed salad and gently toss together to combine. Top with the sliced hard-boiled eggs and garnish with dill, then serve.

Per portion Energy 355kcal/1495kJ; Protein 25g; Carbohydrate 30.8g, of which sugars 22.2g; Fat 15.4g, of which saturates 4.5g; Cholesterol 160mg; Calcium 84mg; Fibre 4.2g; Sodium 1169mg.

Salmon, Potato and Mushroom Bake

This layered bake is a variation of a popular dish in Latvia, where fish, mushrooms and potatoes form the core of the diet. The hint of caraway goes well with the rich salmon and mushrooms, and this is a hearty meal needing just a salad and some rye bread, if you like.

1 Preheat the oven to 180°C/350°F/Gas 4. Heat 75–90ml/5–6 tbsp oil in a large non-stick frying pan over a medium heat. Add the potatoes a few at a time, and cook for 5–8 minutes, or until they are almost tender and lightly browned. (You may need to cook them for a little longer, depending on how thinly you have sliced them.) Remove with a slotted spoon and set aside.

2 Add the butter to the pan and add the mushrooms. Sauté for 4 minutes, or until soft. Season to taste and remove from the pan.

3 Add the remaining oil to the pan and cook the onion rings for 4–5 minutes, or until lightly browned and soft. Line individual serving dishes, or a 20cm/8in square ovenproof dish, with most of the pre-cooked potatoes in a solid layer, overlapping the slices slightly. Spoon over the mushrooms, and then top with the onion rings. Grind the caraway seeds using a mortar and pestle, and sprinkle over the top.

4 Top with the salmon fillets and finish with a layer of the remaining potatoes. Combine the eggs and cream in a bowl and pour over the bake. Sprinkle with the breadcrumbs. Bake individual dishes for 20–25 minutes, and the larger dish for 35–40 minutes, or until golden brown. Serve hot.

Serves 4–6

135ml/4½fl oz/scant ⅔ cup vegetable oil

4 baking potatoes, peeled and thinly sliced

10g/¼oz/½ tbsp butter

300g/11oz/generous 4 cups mushrooms, thinly sliced

1 large onion, finely sliced in rings

1.5ml/¼ tsp caraway seeds

500g/1¼lb thin salmon fillets, bones and skin removed

2 large eggs, beaten

300ml/½ pint/1¼ cups single (light) cream

200g/7oz/3½ cups fresh rye breadcrumbs

salt and ground black pepper

Cook's Tips
• Avoid farmed salmon and Atlantic salmon. The most sustainable choice is wild-caught Alaskan salmon.
• When buying salmon, look for moist, translucent flesh. Fresh salmon will give slightly with finger pressure, and then spring back into shape.

Per portion Energy 689kcal/2877kJ; Protein 27.2g; Carbohydrate 57.6g, of which sugars 7.1g; Fat 40.4g, of which saturates 11.2g; Cholesterol 149mg; Calcium 144mg; Fibre 3.4g; Sodium 422mg.

Estonian Orange and Vodka Gravlax

Gravlax was originally a Swedish dish and there is so much Scandinavian culinary influence in the Baltic that many of the fish dishes involve this way of preparing fish. Normally gravlax is prepared with salmon but here trout is used, which makes a tasty change. Vodka is included in the curing process and gives the gravlax an authentic Baltic flavour. It makes a great accompaniment to many dishes, such as salads and sandwiches, or can be used as a topping for blinis.

1 Lay the trout fillet on a very large piece of clear film (plastic wrap) and pat dry with kitchen paper. Drizzle with the vodka.

2 In a bowl, combine the salt, sugar, mustard and berries. Rub the mixture into the trout flesh. Sprinkle with the orange zest and rub in. Sprinkle over the dill, then press gently on to the fish.

3 Wrap the fish tightly in the clear film (you may need to use some more to get a liquid-tight wrapping). Put the wrapped fish on a tray, cover with a chopping board and then weigh down with kitchen weights or cans. Allow the fish to marinate for 3 days, then remove the clear film and scrape the fish to remove the marinade. Pat the fish dry and slice very thinly. Serve immediately.

Per portion Energy 114kcal/477kJ; Protein 17.5g; Carbohydrate 1.6g, of which sugars 1.6g; Fat 3.4g, of which saturates 0g; Cholesterol 0mg; Calcium 12mg; Fibre 0.1g; Sodium 641mg.

Serves 10 as an appetizer

900g/2lb thick trout fillets, skin on, bones removed

30ml/2 tbsp vodka

45ml/3 tbsp sea salt or coarse salt

45ml/3 tbsp caster (superfine) sugar

5ml/1 tsp mustard powder

15ml/1 tbsp juniper berries, crushed

15ml/1 tbsp grated orange rind

1 large bunch dill, finely chopped

Variations
• Use farmed rainbow trout as a sustainable option.
• To change the flavour to lemon, use lemon zest instead of orange.

Serves 4

2 large baking potatoes, peeled

20g/³⁄₄oz clarified or regular butter

115g/4oz salad leaves

200g/7oz smoked eel, cut into
8 thin strips

For the dill and creamed horseradish

200g/7oz crème fraîche

5ml/1 tsp creamed horseradish

15ml/1 tbsp finely chopped fresh dill

salt and ground black pepper

Smoked Eel on Röstis with Dill and Horseradish

This light dish comes from one of the best restaurants in Riga. Strips of smoked eel top crisp rösti and salad leaves, finished with a dollop of a creamy horseradish and dill dressing. Try the same recipe with smoked haddock or smoked salmon.

1 To make the dill and creamed horseradish, put the crème fraîche in a large bowl with the creamed horseradish and dill. Combine and season with salt and pepper.

2 Grate the potatoes fairly coarsely and put into a colander to drain. Sprinkle them with a little salt to help draw out the excess moisture. Wrap the potato in a piece of muslin (cheesecloth) and squeeze to remove the remaining moisture.

3 Heat the butter in a frying pan over a medium-low heat. Take a large spoonful of the grated potatoes and shape into a round about 7.5cm/3in in diameter. Make three more röstis in the same way. Put into the pan (you may need to cook in batches) and cook for about 5 minutes on each side, or until golden brown. Remove from the pan and keep warm while you cook the remainder.

4 Put a rösti on each serving plate, then top with a handful of the salad leaves. Arrange two strips of the smoked eel on top and garnish with some of the dill and creamed horseradish. Serve immediately.

Per portion Energy 403kcal/1677kJ; Protein 11.8g; Carbohydrate 22.1g, of which sugars 3.4g; Fat 30.4g, of which saturates 17.9g; Cholesterol 143mg; Calcium 55mg; Fibre 1.6g; Sodium 119mg.

Scallops with Black Pudding and Potato, Celery and Apple Mash

This recipe is a modern twist on a classic Estonian recipe using sweet and delicate scallops, topped with black pudding and nestled on a sweet–savoury mash. Estonians love black pudding and the flavour combinations used here contrast well. The dish is light, yet packed with unexpected flavours.

1 To make the mash, put the celery, potato and apple in a pan and cover with water. Bring to the boil and cook until soft. Drain and mash, or pass through a potato ricer. Season, and add a touch of nutmeg and some butter. You need a firm mash so that it will stay in shape when serving. Keep warm.

2 Preheat the oven to 160°C/325°F/Gas 3. Put the black pudding in a roasting pan and roast for 10–12 minutes. Remove and keep warm.

3 Add a smear of oil to a heavy non-stick frying pan or griddle and heat over high heat. Cook the scallops for about 2 minutes on each side, or until golden brown.

4 To serve, make three small heaps of mash, about 45ml/3 tbsp each, on each serving plate, about 5cm/2in apart. Put a scallop on top of each heap, then top with a small pile of the cooked black pudding. Sprinkle with fresh chervil and squeeze a little lemon juice over the top. Season and serve.

Per portion Energy 457kcal/1916kJ; Protein 26.8g; Carbohydrate 38.5g, of which sugars 5.2g; Fat 22.8g, of which saturates 8.9g; Cholesterol 97mg; Calcium 161mg; Fibre 2.2g; Sodium 1087mg.

Serves 4

400g/14oz good-quality, soft black pudding (blood sausage), chopped

extra virgin olive oil, for greasing

12 large scallops

salt and ground black pepper

chopped fresh chervil, to garnish

juice of 1 lemon, to serve

For the mash

4–5 celery sticks, chopped into small pieces

400g/14oz potatoes, peeled and diced

1 large cooking apple, peeled and diced

a pinch of freshly grated nutmeg

knob (pat) of butter (optional)

Variations The most sustainable choice of scallop is farmed bay scallops. Acceptable alternatives are sea scallops from Canada and the US.

Serves 4

200g/7oz raw beetroot (beets), grated

300g/11oz white radish, peeled and grated

115g/4oz carrots, grated

30ml/2 tbsp sour cream

15ml/1 tbsp creamed horseradish

30ml/2 tbsp mayonnaise

45ml/3 tbsp finely chopped fresh dill

115g/4oz white crab meat

grated rind and juice of 1 lemon

115g/4oz small beetroot (beet) leaves

salt and ground black pepper

Variations When choosing crab meat, ensure it is from a sustainable source. Avoid using king crabs, unless they are fished in the USA. The best options are Dungeness and stone crabs; other alternatives are blue crabs and snow crabs.

White Radish, Horseradish and Beetroot Salad with Fresh Crab

This is a Westernized version of an Estonian salad, which uses white crab meat instead of the more common herrings. Young and tender beetroot leaves make a crisp bed for the piquant combination of grated vegetables and horseradish topped with sweet, fresh crab.

1 Wrap the grated beetroot in a piece of muslin (cheesecloth) and squeeze out as much liquid as possible. Put the beetroot into a large bowl and add the grated white radish and carrots.

2 Add the sour cream, creamed horseradish and mayonnaise, then mix well. Sprinkle with the dill and gently stir into the salad. Season to taste and chill until ready to serve.

3 Put the crab meat into a bowl and add the lemon juice and rind. Mix well and season. When ready to serve, put a 12cm/4½in metal ring into the middle of a serving plate, then put a small handful of beetroot salad leaves into the ring. Spoon in the radish, horseradish and beetroot salad, gently pressing down, then remove the ring. Repeat for the remaining plates. Scoop a generous spoonful of the crab meat on to the top of the salads and serve immediately.

Per portion Energy 154kcal/640kJ; Protein 8.4g; Carbohydrate 9.1g, of which sugars 8.4g; Fat 9.6g, of which saturates 2.2g; Cholesterol 31mg; Calcium 90mg; Fibre 3g; Sodium 281mg.

Meat dishes

Stuffing, meat loaves and roasts

When the weather is cold in the Baltic regions, meat, served with potatoes or other root vegetables, makes the perfect hearty meal, whereas in the summer months lighter fish will more often be the preference. It is still common to have families raising their own animals, such as pigs or lambs, and every part of the animal is utilized. So there are numerous traditional recipes for dishes such as jellied pig's head, tripe and tongue terrines. This chapter, however, concentrates on the more popular cuts of meat.

Pork is the most favoured meat. Traditionally, a pig will be slaughtered near to Christmas and the meat will be preserved for use over the following cold months. Minced pork as well as beef is often used to make a filling for dumplings or for stuffings and meat loaves, such as Stuffed Cabbage Leaves or Pork and Cranberry Meat Loaf with Dill Sauce, combined with the traditional spices and flavourings.

In recent times chicken has become affordable and a popular choice, whereas as recently as the 1990s it was expensive and not commonly available. Goose is preferred for Christmas fare and in Lithuania you will find plenty of wild meat dishes on the menu, especially during the hunting season during the autumn and winter, as Lithuanians are keen hunters. Examples given here are Guinea Fowl Kiev and Roast Duck with Elderberry Sauce.

Serves 4

4 skinless chicken breast fillets, about 150g/5¼oz each

45ml/3 tbsp vegetable oil

10g/¼oz/½ tbsp butter

300g/11oz/4 cups wild mushrooms, chopped

6 juniper berries, crushed

1 shallot, grated

115g/4oz/½ cup minced (ground) veal or chicken

1 egg, beaten

60ml/4 tbsp finely chopped fresh parsley

15ml/1 tbsp finely chopped fresh dill

30ml/2 tbsp finely chopped fresh thyme

8 streaky (fatty) bacon rashers (strips)

100ml/3½fl oz/scant ½ cup chicken stock

100ml/3½fl oz/scant ½ cup white wine

30ml/2 tbsp sour cream

30ml/2 tbsp creamed horseradish

salt and ground black pepper

Chicken Breasts Stuffed with Wild Mushrooms and Juniper

During the mushroom season there is a glut of wild mushrooms all over the Baltic, so a wide selection of regional recipes include them. Here they are combined with juniper berries and veal or chicken to make a richly flavoured stuffing for chicken breast fillets. Serve with a wine and cream sauce with a little added zing from the addition of horseradish.

1 Preheat the oven to 180°C/350°F/Gas 4. Put each chicken breast fillet on a board, cover with clear film (plastic wrap) and pound with a meat pounder or a rolling pin until thinned and enlarged. This will make it large enough to stuff easily.

2 Put half the oil and all the butter in a large frying pan and add the mushrooms, then sauté for 5–6 minutes, or until wilted and cooked. Transfer into a bowl and add the juniper berries, shallot, minced veal or chicken, egg and herbs. Combine well and season to taste.

3 Divide the filling among the chicken fillets and roll them up to enclose. Wrap each with two bacon rashers.

4 Heat the remaining oil in a heavy frying pan that can be used in the oven, or a flameproof casserole, over medium-high heat, and add the chicken fillets with the bacon seams down. Cook, turning, to brown the rolls all over, pressing gently at first to seal. Add the stock and white wine, then put the pan in the oven and cook for 30 minutes, or until the chicken is cooked through.

5 Remove the chicken rolls from the pan and leave to rest on a warm serving plate. Put the pan on the stove over a medium heat and simmer to reduce the cooking liquid. Add the sour cream and horseradish, then heat through. Serve the chicken with the sauce.

Per portion Energy 456kcal/1902kJ; Protein 47.3g; Carbohydrate 2.5g, of which sugars 2.1g; Fat 26.9g, of which saturates 7.8g; Cholesterol 154mg; Calcium 74mg; Fibre 1.8g; Sodium 608mg.

Guinea Fowl Kiev

Although made famous by the chefs of Kiev, variations of chicken Kiev are made all across the Baltic States. This is a particularly delicious version that uses guinea fowl. Wild garlic, if it is in season and you can get hold of it, makes a mouthwatering Kiev butter.

Serves 4

4 guinea fowl breast portions, with bone

200g/7oz plain (all-purpose) flour

2 eggs, lightly beaten

300g/11oz dry bread breadcrumbs

75–90ml/5–6 tbsp olive oil

salt and ground black pepper

For the Kiev butter

150g/5oz/10 tbsp butter

30ml/2 tbsp chopped fresh chives

200g/7oz wild garlic leaves, chopped

30ml/2 tbsp chopped fresh parsley

2 garlic cloves, crushed

Variations

• The filling can also be made with a mixture of veal and pork.

• When they are in season, add wild garlic leaves for a more intense flavour, sautéeing them.

1 To make the Kiev butter, put all the ingredients in a food processor or blender and pulse until blended. Season with salt and pepper. Transfer the mixture on to some baking parchment and form into a log shape, then chill to harden.

2 Preheat oven to 200°C/400°F/Gas 6. To prepare the guinea fowl, make a slit in the middle of each breast portion, about 2cm/³⁄₄in deep. Cut about a quarter of the Kiev butter log and put it inside the breast cavity. Overlap the flesh to close the guinea fowl breast portion. Secure with a cocktail stick (toothpick). Then repeat for the remaining portions.

3 Put the flour on to a plate, put the beaten eggs in a shallow bowl, and the breadcrumbs on another plate. Dip the prepared guinea fowl into the flour to coat well, then dip into the eggs. Finally dip in the breadcrumbs to coat completely.

4 Heat the oil in a large frying pan that can be used in the oven, or in a flameproof casserole. Add the Kievs and cook, turning, for 5–6 minutes, or until browned all over.

5 Transfer the kievs to the oven and cook for a further 25–30 minutes, or until cooked through.

Per portion Energy 1046kcal/4383kJ; Protein 48.2g; Carbohydrate 105.4g, of which sugars 3.7g; Fat 50.9g, of which saturates 24g; Cholesterol 235mg; Calcium 230mg; Fibre 5.8g; Sodium 983mg.

Estonian Sweet-and-sour Chicken

Cranberries, mustard and apple add the sweet–sour tones to this unusual oven-cooked dish. In the past, chicken was never particularly common in the Baltic, and during the Communist period it was considered to be a real treat. Today, however, chicken is much more easily available, and this recipe is a new arrival on the culinary scene. Serve with plain boiled potatoes.

1 Preheat the oven to 180°C/350°F/Gas 4. Spread half the butter all over the chicken portions and arrange them in a baking tray. Roast for 30 minutes, basting from time to time.

2 Meanwhile, add the remaining butter to a deep frying pan and cook the onion for 5–8 minutes, or until softened but not browned. Add the apple, sugar, mustard and cranberries. Pour in the chicken stock and simmer for 10 minutes.

3 Pour the mixture over the chicken and return to the oven for another 15 minutes, or until the chicken is cooked through.

Per portion Energy 507kcal/2116kJ; Protein 35.5g; Carbohydrate 21.8g, of which sugars 21.4g; Fat 31.5g, of which saturates 10.9g; Cholesterol 226mg; Calcium 34mg; Fibre 1.4g; Sodium 220mg.

Serves 4

20g/¾oz/1½oz butter

4 chicken leg portions

1 onion, finely sliced

1 apple, grated

45ml/3 tbsp soft light brown sugar

5ml/1 tsp wholegrain mustard

300g/11oz/2¾ cups cranberries

100ml/3½fl oz/scant ½ cup chicken stock

Serves 4

4 duck breast fillets, about 180g/
6⅓oz each

300ml/½ pint/1¼ cups chicken stock

200g/7oz/scant ⅔ cup
elderberry preserve

45ml/3 tbsp elderberry liqueur

15ml/1 tbsp balsamic vinegar

10ml/2 tsp fresh thyme leaves

salt and ground black pepper

Variation This dish also works well
with goose leg or chicken.

Roast Duck with Elderberry Sauce

*Although duck is not a traditional Baltic dish, in recent years it has become
more and more popular. It is usually prepared for special occasions and often
accompanied by fruity sauces, wild berries or preserves, such as the elderberry
preserve used here. Serve with sautéed greens.*

1 Preheat the oven to 180°C/350°F/Gas 4. Heat a heavy frying pan that can be
used in the oven over a medium-high heat. Score the skin of the duck breast fillets
in a criss-cross pattern and season with salt and pepper. Put the duck fillets, skin
side down, in the pan or casserole and cook for 3–4 minutes, or until the fat has
run and the skin is lightly golden. Turn over and repeat on the other side.

2 Transfer the pan or casserole to the oven and cook for 10 minutes, or until the
duck is cooked through. Remove to a warm plate and leave to rest.

3 Put the stock in a small pan over a medium-high heat and add the elderberry
preserve and liqueur. Simmer to reduce to about half, then add the balsamic
vinegar; the sauce should have a syrupy consistency. Season.

4 Slice the duck breast fillets diagonally and arrange on a plate. Pour over some of
the sauce and sprinkle with thyme leaves. Serve the remaining sauce separately.

Per portion Energy 345kcal/1451kJ; Protein 12.5g; Carbohydrate 37.4g, of which sugars 37.4g; Fat
15.3g, of which saturates 4.1g; Cholesterol 89mg; Calcium 14mg; Fibre 0g; Sodium 74mg.

Serves 4

400g/14oz thin veal escalopes
40g/1½oz/3 tbsp butter
1 large shallot, finely chopped
400g/14oz/5½ cups button (white) mushrooms, finely chopped
5ml/1 tsp plain (all-purpose) flour
120ml/4fl oz/½ cup sour cream
120ml/4fl oz/½ cup veal stock
60ml/4 tbsp dry white wine
15ml/1 tbsp chopped parsley, to garnish

Cook's Tip Veal needs very little cooking – so make sure you follow the advised cooking times.

Veal Braised in Sour Cream with Mushrooms and White Wine

This dish is not dissimilar to beef stroganoff, only we are using veal. Tender veal is an ideal meat for a quick meal. Here it is cut into strips and quickly fried, then served with a creamy mushroom and wine sauce. Serve with boiled potatoes.

1 Put the veal escalopes on a board, cover with clear film (plastic wrap) and pound with a meat pounder or a rolling pin until very thin.

2 Slice into thin strips. Heat a third of the butter in a non-stick frying pan over a medium heat. Add the shallot and cook for 5 minutes, or until soft, then add the mushrooms, cooking them until lightly browned. The mushrooms will release some liquid, so cook until this liquid has evaporated. Remove from the pan and set aside.

3 Melt half the remaining butter in the same pan and gently cook the veal strips for 5 minutes.

4 In a small pan, melt the remaining butter and sprinkle in the flour, stirring constantly. Very slowly, add the sour cream and veal stock, stirring constantly. Continue cooking over a low-medium heat until the sauce has thickened. Add the onion and mushroom mixture, the veal and wine, and cook for 10 more minutes. Serve with a garnish of parsley.

Per portion Energy 274kcal/1142kJ; Protein 25.7g; Carbohydrate 3.8g, of which sugars 2.3g; Fat 16.4g, of which saturates 9.9g; Cholesterol 93mg; Calcium 46mg; Fibre 1.4g; Sodium 153mg.

Pan-fried Veal with Mustard and Dill Sauce

In this modern Estonian recipe, usually served in the spring when veal is available, veal is pan-fried and then served with a Madeira, mustard and dill sauce. It is a quick, satisfying meal that just needs spring vegetables and boiled new potatoes as an accompaniment.

1 Put the veal cutlets on a board and flatten a little using a meat pounder or a rolling pin. Dust with the flour and season with salt and pepper.

2 Heat the butter and 5ml/1 tsp oil in a large frying pan over a medium heat, and cook the veal cutlets for 5–8 minutes on each side, until golden brown. Remove from the pan and keep warm.

3 Add the Madeira and chicken stock to the frying pan and cook until reduced, stirring frequently. Add the mustard and dill, and cook for 3 more minutes. Serve the veal cutlets with the sauce.

Per portion Energy 457kcal/1921kJ; Protein 63.3g; Carbohydrate 10.1g, of which sugars 1.5g; Fat 16.6g, of which saturates 1.6g; Cholesterol 218mg; Calcium 33mg; Fibre 0.6g; Sodium 284mg.

Serves 4

4 veal cutlets, about 200g/7oz each

10ml/2 tsp plain (all-purpose) flour

10g/¼oz/½ tbsp butter

30ml/2 tbsp vegetable oil

60ml/4 tbsp Madeira

200ml/7fl oz/scant 1 cup chicken stock

15ml/1 tbsp wholegrain mustard

30ml/2 tbsp finely chopped fresh dill

salt and ground black pepper

Variation The mustard and dill sauce can also be used as a tasty accompaniment to vegetable dishes.

60ml/4 tbsp vegetable oil

1 large onion, finely chopped

200g/7oz/scant 3 cups mushrooms, chopped

300g/11oz/1⅓ cups minced (ground) veal

300g/11oz/1⅓ cups minced (ground) pork

30ml/2 tbsp chopped fresh dill

75ml/5 tbsp toasted breadcrumbs

1 large (US extra large) egg, beaten

100ml/3½fl oz/scant ½ cup chicken stock

150ml/¼ pint/⅔ cup sour cream

5ml/1 tsp mild mustard

30ml/2 tbsp (extra) finely chopped fresh dill

salt and ground black pepper

Pork and Veal Patties with Sour Cream and Mustard Sauce

These meat patties, called kurzemes, are one of Latvia's best-known dishes. They are prepared with a combination of mixed meat, often veal and pork, but they can also include chopped ham. Sautéed mushrooms are added to the meat mixture here to give the patties even more flavour and they are served with a sour cream sauce.

1 Heat 15ml/1 tbsp oil in a frying pan over a medium heat and cook the onion for 3–4 minutes, or until slightly golden, remove using a slotted spoon and set aside.

2 Add the mushrooms to the pan and cook for 4–5 minutes, or until soft; use a little more oil if required. Remove using a slotted spoon and set aside.

3 Put the veal into a large mixing bowl, and add the pork, dill, half the onions and half the mushrooms. Season with salt and pepper, and mix well.

4 Add the breadcrumbs and egg, and mix again. Shape the mixture into flat patties. Heat the remaining oil in a large, heavy non-stick pan over a medium heat. Now add the meat patties and cook for 10–12 minutes on both sides, or until the meat is browned; you may need to cook them in batches.

5 Remove the cooked patties from the pan and keep warm. Pour the stock into the pan and add the remaining half of the sautéed onions and mushrooms. Cook over a medium-high heat, stirring, for 5 minutes, or until reduced. Adjust the seasoning.

6 When the sauce is reduced by half, add the sour cream and mustard. Cook gently for 3 more minutes, then add the dill. Serve the meat patties with the sauce over the top.

Per portion Energy 247kcal/1028kJ; Protein 15.3g; Carbohydrate 10.2g, of which sugars 2.5g; Fat 16.4g, of which saturates 5.4g; Cholesterol 76mg; Calcium 55mg; Fibre 1.1g; Sodium 133mg.

Stuffed Cabbage Leaves

A lean minced beef and rice stuffing, with a hint of paprika and dill, is enclosed in tender Savoy cabbage leaves in this typical Baltic dish. For a traditional meal, serve with a fruit preserve, such as a lingonberry conserve.

1 Fill a large pan with boiling water and put over a high heat. Discard the outer cabbage leaves and cut out the core. Drop the cabbage into the boiling water, making sure that it is covered. Add salt and boil for 2–3 minutes, or until the leaves are tender but still bright green.

2 Remove from the water and take out the leaves, choosing 16 good ones. Put the remainder to one side.

3 Put the minced beef, cooked rice, dill, egg and paprika in a large bowl and combine well. Season to taste with salt and pepper. Preheat the oven to 180°C/350°F/Gas 4.

4 Make the cabbage rolls using the leaves that you have selected. Put a generous tablespoonful of meat mixture into the centre of each leaf. Roll up to about halfway, starting with the root end, then fold in the sides and continue rolling to the top. Repeat with the remaining leaves and meat mixture.

5 Arrange some of the discarded leaves over the base of an ovenproof dish and lay the stuffed cabbage rolls on top, next to each other with the fold side down. Add the chicken stock and cover the dish with foil. Cook in the oven for 30 minutes. Remove the foil, baste with the cooking liquid and cook for a further 10–12 minutes, or until lightly browned. Serve the stuffed cabbage leaves hot or cold, accompanied by a fruit preserve.

Serves 4

1 Savoy cabbage

675g/1½lb lean minced (ground) beef

200g/7oz/scant 2 cups boiled plain long grain rice (90g/3½oz/½ cup raw rice)

30ml/2 tbsp finely chopped fresh dill

1 egg

2.5ml/½ tsp paprika

600ml/1 pint/2½ cups chicken stock

salt and ground black pepper

fruit preserve, to serve

Cook's Tips

• When preparing the cabbage, carefully remove the leaves by pulling on the thick ends and peeling down. Remove and set aside 16 of the leaves that look big enough to fold around the filling.

• Stuffed cabbage leaves freeze wonderfully for future meals.

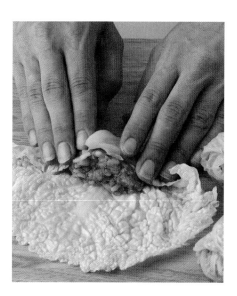

Per portion Energy 517kcal/2153kJ; Protein 37.4g; Carbohydrate 25.8g, of which sugars 7.6g; Fat 29.3g, of which saturates 12g; Cholesterol 159mg; Calcium 135mg; Fibre 3.8g; Sodium 177mg.

Lithuanian Hussar Roast

This hussar's roast is the best roast beef you will ever taste. With a myriad of contrasting flavours, such as thyme and dill, horseradish and mustard, vegetables and rhubarb, the roast has added richness from smoked pork cubes cooked in the pot. The dish is also popular in Poland. Serve with potatoes and steamed beans.

1 Preheat the oven to 180°C/350°F/Gas 4. Heat the vegetable oil in a large, flameproof casserole over a high heat. Season the beef with salt and pepper, then cook for 2–3 minutes on each side, or until lightly brown. Add the smoked pork cubes and cook, turning, for 2 more minutes.

2 Add the onion, carrot, celery and rhubarb. Season, then add the wine, stock, bay leaf, thyme, dill, peppercorns and cloves. Stir, making sure that some of the mixture goes beneath the meat. Put the casserole in the oven and cook for 1 hour. Remove and stir in the grated horseradish and mustard to the cooking juices.

3 Cook for a further 45 minutes in the oven. Remove and leave to rest for 10–15 minutes. Slice the meat and serve with the cooking juices and vegetables.

Per portion Energy 379kcal/1580kJ; Protein 41.7g; Carbohydrate 2.5g, of which sugars 2.2g; Fat 20.7g, of which saturates 7.2g; Cholesterol 101mg; Calcium 44mg; Fibre 1g; Sodium 285mg.

Serves 6

30ml/2 tbsp vegetable oil

1kg/2¼lb sirloin of beef, in one piece

115g/4oz smoked pork or gammon (smoked or cured ham), cubed

1 large onion, diced

1 carrot, diced

2 celery sticks, diced

2 rhubarb sticks, diced

150ml/¼ pint/⅔ cup white wine

150ml/¼ pint/⅔ cup beef stock

1 bay leaf

8 thyme sprigs

6 dill sprigs

8 peppercorns

3 cloves

15ml/1 tbsp grated horseradish

15ml/1 tbsp made mustard

salt and ground black pepper

Serves 6–8

3kg/6lb 9oz pork loin on the bone

30ml/2 tbsp sea salt or coarse salt

15ml/1 tbsp juniper berries, crushed

6 ready-to-eat dried apricots, halved

6 large ready-to-eat prunes, pitted

2 apples, quartered and cored

1 large onion, quartered

about 300ml/½ pint/1¼ cups chicken stock

ground black pepper

Variation Replace the pork loin with roast beef or veal. The sweet and sour flavours of the berries, apricots and prunes also combine well with these meats.

Roasted Pork with Juniper Berries

Fruits are a traditional accompaniment to pork in many cuisines, but in this traditional Estonian roast the pork is cooked with apricots, prunes and apples, which absorb the juices and make a luscious accompaniment. Serve with roast potatoes and sauerkraut.

1 Sprinkle the pork with salt, juniper berries and ground black pepper, then rub these flavourings into the meat. Put into a roasting pan, cover and chill for 4–8 hours.

2 Preheat the oven to 180°C/350°F/Gas 4. Arrange the apricots, prunes, apples and onion around and under the meat, then add the stock. Roast for about 3 hours, or until cooked through with no pink juices. The exact roasting time will depend on the size of the joint; it will need roughly 25 minutes per 450g/1lb plus 25 minutes extra. Top up with more stock if it reduces too much. You will find that the meat releases some fat and cooking juices anyway.

3 Remove the meat to a warm plate and allow to rest for 20 minutes in a warm place. Carve and serve accompanied by the apricots, prunes and apples.

Per portion Energy 802kcal/3343kJ; Protein 59.8g; Carbohydrate 13.1g, of which sugars 12.3g; Fat 57.2g, of which saturates 21g; Cholesterol 184mg; Calcium 52mg; Fibre 2.3g; Sodium 170mg.

Cook's Tip The eggs must be properly hard-boiled, as they will need to hold their shape during the rest of the cooking.

Serves 6

15ml/1 tbsp vegetable oil, plus extra for greasing

1 onion, finely chopped

2 garlic cloves, crushed

1kg/2½lb/5 cups minced (ground) pork

2 small eggs, beaten

60ml/4 tbsp fresh breadcrumbs

60ml/4 tbsp frozen or fresh cranberries

3 hard-boiled eggs, peeled

salt and ground black pepper

For the sauce

60ml/4 tbsp sour cream

30ml/2 tbsp mayonnaise

5ml/1 tsp finely chopped fresh dill

1.5ml/¼ tsp mustard

2.5ml/½ tsp honey

Pork and Cranberry Meat Loaf with Dill Sauce

This is a variation on a much-loved Lithuanian meat loaf recipe. It includes cranberries, which are the perfect flavour partner to pork, and the loaf encloses hard-boiled eggs. The loaf is a wonderful meal served either hot or cold and it should be accompanied by a dill and mustard sauce. Serve with potatoes or bread and a salad.

1 Heat the oil in a non-stick frying pan over a medium heat and cook the onion and garlic for 2–3 minutes, or until beginning to soften. Put the pan to one side and allow to cool.

2 Put the pork into a large bowl, and mix in the onion and garlic. Add the beaten eggs and breadcrumbs. Mix together well.

3 Add the cranberries to the bowl and season to taste. Combine gently so that you don't break them up.

4 Preheat the oven to 180°C/350°F/Gas 4 and lightly oil a 1 litre/1¾ pint/4 cup loaf tin (pan). Spread half the meat mixture in the middle of the pan in an oval shape, and then arrange the hard-boiled eggs on top, equally spaced from one another, in a row right down the centre.

5 Cover with the remaining meat mixture, making sure that the eggs are well sealed. Brush with a little oil and cook in the oven for about 1 hour, or until golden brown and cooked through.

6 To make the sauce, put all the ingredients in a bowl, season and mix well. Serve the meat loaf warm or cold, accompanied by the dill sauce.

Per portion Energy 494kcal/2060kJ; Protein 39.5g; Carbohydrate 12g, of which sugars 3.7g; Fat 32.6g, of which saturates 9.9g; Cholesterol 282mg; Calcium 85mg; Fibre 1.3g; Sodium 297mg.

Baltic Baked Ham

A real tradition in the Baltic States, baked ham is often prepared at a time of family celebration. Favourite spices are rubbed into the joint, then apple and mustard are added to give the meat a wonderful flavour. Serve with rye bread.

1 Preheat the oven to 180°C/350°F/Gas 4. Put the cooking apple in a small pan with 15ml/1 tbsp water and cook over a medium heat until very soft. Mash to a purée or use a blender. Set aside.

2 Cut off the skin from the ham and score the fat in a diamond pattern. Put the crushed juniper berries in a bowl and add the cloves, salt and pepper. Mix well. Rub the mixture into the scored fat.

3 Put the mustard and 45ml/3 tbsp of the apple purée into a bowl and mix together, then spread all over the ham. Put the ham in a deep roasting pan and pour in the apple juice. Roast for 2 hours, basting occasionally.

4 Add the prunes and Marsala to the pan and cook for a further 45 minutes, basting again. Remove the meat from the roasting pan and leave on a warm plate to rest for 10–15 minutes. Slice and serve hot with the prunes and Marsala sauce.

Per portion Energy 345kcal/1444kJ; Protein 35.6g; Carbohydrate 11.8g, of which sugars 11.8g; Fat 15.1g, of which saturates 5g; Cholesterol 46mg; Calcium 25mg; Fibre 1.3g; Sodium 1766mg.

Serves 10

1 cooking apple, peeled, cored and cut into chunks

4.5–5kg/10–11lb leg of ham (on the bone)

20 juniper berries, crushed

20 cloves, crushed

2.5ml/$\frac{1}{2}$ tsp salt

1.5ml/$\frac{1}{4}$ tsp ground black pepper

30ml/2 tbsp wholegrain mustard

300ml/$\frac{1}{2}$ pint/1$\frac{1}{4}$ cups apple juice

200g/7oz large ready-to-eat pitted prunes

200ml/7fl oz/scant 1 cup Marsala

Serves 6

30ml/2 tbsp plain (all-purpose) flour

4 lamb shanks, about 200g/7oz each

30ml/2 tbsp vegetable oil

2 small onions, finely chopped

finely grated rind of 2 lemons

1 small bunch parsley, leaves
finely chopped

4 bay leaves

2 carrots, diced

2 large potatoes, peeled and diced

800ml/27fl oz/scant 3$\frac{1}{4}$ cups
lamb stock

150ml/$\frac{1}{4}$ pint/$\frac{2}{3}$ cup thick sour cream

salt and ground black pepper

Estonian Lamb Shanks in Sour Cream Sauce

In this adaptation of an old Estonian recipe, lamb shanks are casseroled with root vegetables, lemon juice and parsley for a robust meal. Sour cream thickens the cooking juices, making a rich sauce to accompany the lamb.

1 Preheat the oven to 180°C/350°F/Gas 4. Put the flour in a plastic bag and add salt and pepper. Drop in the lamb shanks and shake the bag to dust them evenly. Heat the oil in a deep flameproof casserole, and brown the shanks for about 10 minutes. Remove and keep warm.

2 Add the onions to the casserole, and cook for 5 minutes, or until soft, then return the lamb to the casserole. Add the lemon rind, half the parsley, the bay leaves, carrots, potatoes and stock. Season and cover, then cook in the oven for 1$\frac{1}{2}$ hours. Remove from the oven, stir in the sour cream and sprinkle with the remaining parsley. Serve.

Per portion Energy 489kcal/2034kJ; Protein 21g; Carbohydrate 19.9g, of which sugars 5.7g; Fat 36.8g, of which saturates 16.6g; Cholesterol 98mg; Calcium 125mg; Fibre 3.4g; Sodium 100mg.

Desserts and baking

Kissel, cheesecake and pashka

The cuisines of the Baltic do not have a great tradition of desserts because savoury dishes are preferred to sweet ones, so usually fresh fruit is eaten to finish a meal. However, there are some mouthwatering desserts for special occasions. Creamy desserts, such as mousses, creams or kissels – made from seasonal fruits – are great favourites. Berries, when in season, are made into preserves to serve with pancakes or as fillings for cakes and toppings for desserts.

Many of the recipes in this chapter are traditional ones given a modern twist. Latvian desserts tend to be simple and frequently include fruit – as a topping for cheesecakes, for example. Another Latvian favourite is the bubert: a delicious semolina pudding enriched with ground almonds.

In Estonia it is the traditional cheesecake that people most love to eat, such as the Apple and Almond Cheesecake given here. The chapter also includes a recipe for the famous Russian Easter Cake, paskha, made from curd cheese and sour cream, candied fruit peels and glacé fruits – a popular seasonal cake also enjoyed in the Baltic States. There are hundreds of varieties of homemade biscuits eaten in the region, and a few are included, such as the crunchy Rye, Poppy Seed and Honey Cookies or the Lithuanian Caraway and Honey Cookies. The chapter also includes soda breads flavoured with fennel or lightened with cream cheese.

Rhubarb and Berry Rye Crumble

Crumbles are delicious, cosy and heartwarming. This one is a variation of an Estonian pudding of berries and rye. Easy to make, it tastes best with an early crop of sweet blackberries that have ripened in the late-summer sun.

1 Preheat the oven to 180°C/350°F/Gas 4. Put the rhubarb and berries in a large pan and add 50g/2oz/¼ cup of the sugar. Heat gently over a medium heat, stirring constantly. Simmer for 3–5 minutes, or until the rhubarb is just tender, then remove from the heat.

2 Put the remaining sugar, the butter and rye flour into a food processor and pulse until the mixture resembles chunky breadcrumbs. Alternatively, rub the butter into the flour in a bowl by hand or using a pastry (cookie) cutter, then stir in the sugar. Set aside.

3 Put the rye bread into the food processor or a blender and pulse to make breadcrumbs. Stir the rye breadcrumbs into the flour mixture.

4 Pour the rhubarb mixture into a large ovenproof dish. Top generously with the breadcrumb mixture and bake for 20–25 minutes, or until crispy. Serve hot or cold.

Per portion Energy 208kcal/878kJ; Protein 3g; Carbohydrate 37.3g, of which sugars 21.5g; Fat 6.2g, of which saturates 3.8g; Cholesterol 16mg; Calcium 83mg; Fibre 3.6g; Sodium 138mg.

Serves 6–8

400g/14oz rhubarb, cut into 2cm/¾in pieces

200g/7oz/scant 2 cups blackberries or blueberries

150g/5oz/¾ cup caster (superfine) sugar

55g/2oz/¼ cup cold butter, cubed

100g/3½oz/scant 1 cup rye flour

115g/4oz rye bread

sour cream, to serve

Variation Use brioche breadcrumbs in place of the rye bread for a less rustic, more refined, topping.

Serves 4–6

200g/7oz white bread slices,
crust removed

150ml/¼ pint/⅔ cup single (light) cream

50g/2oz/¼ cup butter, melted

4 eggs, separated

45ml/3 tbsp caster (superfine) sugar

200g/7oz sliced dried apples,
roughly chopped

50g/2oz/scant ½ cup raisins

75g/2oz/¼ cup flaked (sliced) almonds

Variation Adding a grated apple to the dry apple and raisin mixture makes the pudding even more moist.

Baltic Bread and Apple Pudding

Here is a simple recipe for a Latvian bread pudding that uses, unusually for a Baltic recipe, white bread and not rye. Serve with a spoonful of homemade apricot preserve, or a good-quality bought one.

1 Preheat the oven to 180°C/350°F/Gas 4 and grease a 15 x 20cm/6 x 8in ovenproof dish. Process the bread in a food processor or blender until you have breadcrumbs. Transfer into a bowl and add the cream and butter, mixing well.

2 In another bowl, whisk the egg yolks and sugar until light and creamy. Fold the apples and raisins into the whisked egg and sugar mixture. Add this to the breadcrumb mixture, and combine well.

3 Put the egg whites into a clean, grease-free bowl and whisk until they form stiff peaks. Stir a spoonful of the whites into the breadcrumb mixture to lighten it, then fold in the remaining whites. Pour into the prepared dish.

4 Sprinkle with the almonds and bake for 25–30 minutes, or until golden and firm.

Per portion Energy 379kcal/1585kJ; Protein 10.6g; Carbohydrate 34.9g, of which sugars 19g; Fat 23g, of which saturates 9.2g; Cholesterol 160mg; Calcium 119mg; Fibre 2.1g; Sodium 303mg.

Latvian Semolina and Almond Pudding with Rhubarb

In Latvia and Estonia, a semolina pudding, called bubert, is a popular midweek dessert because it is so easy to make. Ground almonds enrich this creamy pudding, which is made using soya milk because it has an extra-rich taste, although traditionally the recipe would use whole milk.

Serves 4

30ml/2 tbsp blanched almonds

500ml/17fl oz/2¼ cups soya milk (or whole milk)

1 vanilla pod (bean), split lengthways

30ml/2 tbsp fine semolina

2 large (US extra large) eggs, separated

75ml/5 tbsp caster (superfine) sugar

45ml/3 tbsp ground almonds

300g/11oz rhubarb, cut into 3cm/1¼in pieces

Variation When they are in season, use fresh berries instead of rhubarb, such as redcurrants or cranberries.
Use them to prepare a fruit coulis, a fruit soup or stewed fruit. Any of these will be an excellent combination with the silky semolina.

1 Put the almonds in a dry pan and toast over a medium-high heat, tossing regularly, for 2–3 minutes, or until golden brown. Pour the milk into a pan. Scrape the seeds of the vanilla pod and add to the milk, together with the pod itself. Bring to the boil, then remove the pod.

2 Whisk in the semolina, stirring constantly to avoid lumps forming. Put the egg yolks and sugar into another bowl and whisk until light and creamy. Gradually add the hot semolina to the eggs and 45ml/3 tbsp sugar, whisking constantly.

3 Return the mixture to a clean pan and cook over a low heat until thickened. Remove from the heat and allow to cool slightly. Stir in the ground almonds.

4 Put the egg whites into a clean, grease-free bowl and whisk until the eggs form soft peaks. Stir a spoonful into the semolina to lighten the mixture, then gently fold in the remainder.

5 Put the rhubarb in a pan with the remaining sugar and 30–45ml/2–3 tbsp water, which should be just enough to stop it sticking to the pan. Simmer gently for 8 minutes. Serve the semolina pudding topped with the stewed rhubarb and sprinkled with the toasted almonds.

Per portion Energy 223kcal/929kJ; Protein 12.2g; Carbohydrate 8.7g, of which sugars 2.4g; Fat 15.5g, of which saturates 2g; Cholesterol 95mg; Calcium 147mg; Fibre 2.6g; Sodium 81mg.

Estonian Apple and Almond Cheesecake

This isn't a typical cheesecake, more of a cheese and apple pie. It has plenty of flavour and is perfect served with a summer berry coulis. This is one of the most common desserts in the Baltics, often made with homemade cheese.

1 Preheat the oven to 180°C/350°F/Gas 4. Butter and line a 20 x 30cm/8 x 12in cake tin (pan). Put the cream cheese and ricotta cheese in a large bowl and mix well. Add the egg yolks one at a time, stirring each into the cheese mixture.

2 Sprinkle the semolina flour over the top and stir in, then add the ground almonds, followed by the sour cream and sugar.

3 Put the egg whites into a clean, grease-free bowl and whisk until they form stiff peaks. Stir two large spoonfuls into the cheese mixture, then fold in the remainder.

4 Put the apples into a large bowl. Add the lemon juice and rind, and mix well to coat. (The juice will prevent the apples from discoloration and add flavour.) Add the apples to the cheese mixture and fold in. Transfer into the prepared tin and sprinkle with the flaked almonds. Bake for 40 minutes, or until the top is golden brown.

5 Put the berries in a small pan with the sugar and 15–30ml/1–2 tbsp water. Simmer for 5–6 minutes, or until just softened. Purée the berries in a blender, pass through a fine sieve (strainer) and cool. Serve the cheesecake with the berry coulis.

Per portion Energy 500kcal/2080kJ; Protein 12.8g; Carbohydrate 30.1g, of which sugars 22.3g; Fat 37.5g, of which saturates 16.9g; Cholesterol 153mg; Calcium 124mg; Fibre 2.4g; Sodium 145mg.

Serves 8

250g/9oz/generous 1 cup
cream cheese

250g/9oz/generous 1 cup
ricotta cheese

4 eggs, separated

75g/3oz/²⁄₃ cup semolina flour

30ml/2 tbsp ground almonds

200ml/7fl oz/scant 1 cup sour cream

115g/4oz/generous ²⁄₃ cup caster
(superfine) sugar

5 eating apples, peeled, cored and
thinly sliced

grated rind and juice of 1 lemon

115g/4oz/1 cup flaked (sliced) almonds

250g/9oz/generous 2 cups berries (any
that are in season)

10ml/2 tsp sugar

Serves 6–8

225g/8oz/1 cup creamy, thick
goat's cheese

75g/3oz/$\frac{1}{3}$ cup soft light brown sugar

3 eggs, lightly beaten

120ml/4fl oz/$\frac{1}{2}$ cup crème fraîche

400g/14oz/2$\frac{1}{3}$ cups raspberries

30ml/2 tbsp caster (superfine) sugar

Variation For a creamier texture, use cream cheese or curd cheese, or a mixture of the two.

Goat's Cheese Cheesecakes with Raspberry Sauce

Cheesecakes are much loved in the Baltic and there are many different variations to be found. This one, from Riga, is unusual in its use of goat's cheese and it has a thick and fragrant raspberry sauce to drizzle over the top.

1 Preheat the oven to 180°C/350°F/Gas 4. Butter six ramekin dishes. Put the goat's cheese and sugar in a bowl and whisk together until light and fluffy, using an electric mixer, if you like.

2 Gradually add the beaten eggs and continue whisking. The mixture will be fairly liquid. Add the crème fraîche and beat for 1 more minute.

3 Pour the mixture into the ramekin dishes, and put into a roasting pan. Half-fill the pan with warm water, then put into the oven. Cook the cheesecakes for 10 minutes. Turn off the oven, leaving the cheesecakes in the oven to cool slowly. In 1 hour they should be completely set. Remove and set aside.

4 Meanwhile, put the raspberries in a pan with the sugar and cook over a medium heat for 3–5 minutes, or until slightly thickened. Cool. Serve the cheesecakes with the raspberry sauce.

Per portion Energy 239kcal/997kJ; Protein 9.4g; Carbohydrate 16.7g, of which sugars 16.6g; Fat 15.5g, of which saturates 9.7g; Cholesterol 114mg; Calcium 76mg; Fibre 1.3g; Sodium 201mg.

Serves 8–12

165g/5½oz/11 tbsp butter, softened

grated rind of 1 lemon and 1 orange

150g/5oz/¾ cup caster (superfine) sugar

2 large (US extra large) eggs

900g/2lb/2 cups curd cheese

200ml/7fl oz/scant 1 cup sour cream

30ml/2 tbsp finely chopped candied lemon peel

30ml/2 tbsp finely chopped candied orange peel

60ml/4 tbsp sultanas (golden raisins)

30ml/2 tbsp chopped almonds

30ml/2 tbsp glacé (candied) cherries, sliced

30ml/2 tbsp glacé (candied) pineapple, chopped

a large sheet of white muslin (cheesecloth)

To decorate

30 whole glacé (candied) cherries

30ml/2 tbsp slivered almonds

20 thin strips of candied orange peel

Variation Make the pashka in another shape by using a loaf tin (pan) or a square tin.

Estonian Easter Cake

Paskha is the name for this traditional cake prepared for Easter. It is made from cheese and dry fruits, and is very rich. Normally a special paskha mould would be used, but as these are hard to source, you can use a round cake tin instead, or an even better alternative is a clean flowerpot. This Easter cake can also be made in individual portions.

1 Put the butter in a large bowl and add the orange and lemon rind and the sugar. Beat with a wooden spoon or an electric mixer until smooth, light and fluffy. Add the eggs one at a time, beating well after each addition.

2 Beat in the curd cheese and sour cream. Add the candied peels, the sultanas, almonds and the chopped cherries and pineapple. Mix well.

3 Line a paskha mould, loose-based cake tin (pan) or clean flowerpot with a large piece of muslin (cheesecloth), leaving plenty overhanging the side of the tin. Try to line the mould as smoothly as you can to avoid creases, as they will show up on the finished cake.

4 Pour the cheese and fruit mixture into the mould, tapping to make sure that there are no air pockets. Bring over the overhanging muslin to enclose the mixture. Put a small plate on top, then weight down with cans. Chill overnight. Some excess liquid will drain off the cake.

5 Next day, remove the weights and plate. If you are using a paskha mould, unmoulding is easy, as the sides come apart, but if you are using a cake tin or flowerpot, unfold the top of the muslin, then put a serving plate on top of the cake and invert on to the serving plate. Carefully remove the cake tin or flowerpot and unpeel the muslin.

6 Decorate the cake with glacé cherries, almonds and strips of peel. Serve cold.

Per portion Energy 349kcal/1455kJ; Protein 13.5g; Carbohydrate 26.2g, of which sugars 26.2g; Fat 22.9g, of which saturates 13.8g; Cholesterol 91mg; Calcium 134mg; Fibre 0.6g; Sodium 468mg.

Latvian Alexander Cake

This cake was created in honour of Tsar Alexander – a famed gourmand – when he visited Riga. There are a number of different versions, some more difficult than others, but this recipe has been simplified so that it can be made easily at home. Buttery pastry encloses a layer of homemade preserves, and the cake is topped with lemon icing.

1 Put the flour, sugar and cubed butter into a large bowl. Working with your fingertips, combine the mixture until it forms rough breadcrumbs.

2 Add the vanilla extract and yogurt, just a little at a time, working with your fingers. Transfer the mixture on to a floured surface and knead the pastry until you get a smooth dough.

3 Roll the dough into a large ball and put into a bowl, cover with clear film (plastic wrap) and chill for 1 hour.

4 Preheat the oven to 150°C/300°F/Gas 2. Line two baking sheets with baking parchment. Rest the pastry at room temperature for approximately 15 minutes. Divide into two pieces and roll each piece into thin 20cm/8in squares. Prick the dough to stop it blistering.

5 Put each piece of pastry on to a baking sheet. Bake for 20 minutes, or until golden brown. Move to a wire rack and allow to cool.

6 Spread one of the layers with the preserve and top with the other pastry layer. To make the icing, put the icing sugar in a bowl and stir in the lemon juice, adding a few tablespoons of water until you have a smooth icing.

7 Spread the icing over the top of the cake in a thin layer and sprinkle with the lemon rind. Traditionally the cake is cut into diamond shapes before serving.

Makes 30–40 pieces

375g/13oz plain (all-purpose) flour, plus extra for dusting

50g/2oz/¼ cup caster (superfine) sugar

250g/9oz/generous 1 cup chilled butter, cubed

15ml/1 tbsp vanilla extract

45ml/3 tbsp thick natural (plain) yogurt

150g/5½oz/generous ½ cup apricot or blackcurrant preserve

For the icing

125g/4½oz/1⅛ cups icing (confectioners') sugar

15ml/1 tbsp lemon juice

grated rind of 1 lemon

Variations A more traditional filling for these Latvian cakes is a raspberry or cranberry preserve.

Per portion Energy 105kcal/441kJ; Protein 1g; Carbohydrate 14.4g, of which sugars 7.3g; Fat 5.2g, of which saturates 3.4g; Cholesterol 14mg; Calcium 19mg; Fibre 0.3g; Sodium 49mg.

Makes 30–40

1.5ml/¼ tsp cardamom seeds

4 large (US extra large) egg whites

250g/9oz/generous 2 cups icing (confectioners') sugar

115g/4oz/1 cup ground almonds

200ml/7fl oz/scant 1 cup double (heavy) cream, whipped

200g/7oz/scant 2 cups fresh berries, chopped if large

30ml/2 tbsp berry jam

Variation Replace the cardamom seeds with vanilla extract for a different flavour.

Fresh Berry, Almond and Cardamom Macaroons

During the summer, berries are abundant in the Baltic regions. You can use any berry you like to make these gorgeous macaroons, which are lightly flavoured with cardamom and filled with fresh berries and jam.

1 Preheat the oven to 200°C/400°F/Gas 6 and line two large baking sheets with baking parchment. Grind the cardamom seeds finely using a mortar and pestle.

2 Put the egg whites into a clean, grease-free bowl and whisk until they form stiff peaks. Using a wooden spoon, slowly and gently fold in the icing sugar a little at a time. Fold in the almonds and cardamom. You should have a smooth mixture.

3 Using a teaspoon, spoon dollops of the mixture on to the baking parchment, about 5cm/2in apart. Bake for 8–10 minutes, or until golden. Leave the macaroons to cool on the tray.

4 Combine the cream, berries and jam, and use the cooled mixture to make macaroon sandwiches.

Per portion Energy 69kcal/289kJ; Protein 1.1g; Carbohydrate 7.6g, of which sugars 7.6g; Fat 4.3g, of which saturates 1.6g; Cholesterol 7mg; Calcium 15mg; Fibre 0.4g; Sodium 9mg.

Lithuanian Caraway and Honey Cookies

Lemon and caraway flavour these light cookies from Lithuania. They are made in almost every Lithuanian household; every family has their own recipe – but honey is always a consistent ingredient. They are often served with cheese at the end of a meal, as well as for a sweet snack.

1 Put the butter and sugar in a large bowl and cream together, using an electric mixer if you like, until the mixture is smooth and pale. Add the honey and mix again.

2 Add the egg, caraway seeds, lemon juice and rind. Mix well, then sift in the flour and baking powder and gently fold in.

3 Transfer the mixture on to a floured surface and work to a firm dough. Form into a sausage shape, about 30cm/12in long, and wrap in baking parchment. Chill until firm.

4 Preheat the oven to 180°C/350°F/Gas 4 and line a baking sheet with baking parchment. Unwrap the dough, and cut off slices about 5mm/¼in thick. Put them on the prepared baking sheet, spaced apart. Bake for 10 minutes, or until golden. Cool briefly on the baking sheet, then transfer to a wire rack to cool completely.

Per portion Energy 61kcal/255kJ; Protein 0.8g; Carbohydrate 10.2g, of which sugars 4.9g; Fat 2.1g, of which saturates 1.3g; Cholesterol 10mg; Calcium 13mg; Fibre 0.2g; Sodium 19mg.

Make 45–50

115g/4oz/½ cup butter, softened

225g/8oz/generous 1 cup caster (superfine) sugar

5ml/1 tsp honey

1 large (US extra large) egg, beaten

15g/½oz caraway seeds

grated rind and juice of 1 lemon

350g/10½oz/2½ cups plain (all-purpose) flour, plus extra for dusting

2.5ml/½ tsp baking powder

Cook's Tip Prepare a thick chocolate sauce and drizzle over the cookies before serving.

Makes 45–50

200ml/7fl oz/scant 1 cup golden (light corn) syrup

185g/6½oz/scant 1 cup caster (superfine) sugar

5ml/1 tsp ground cinnamon

2.5ml/½ tsp ground cloves

5ml/1 tsp ground cardamom

5ml/1 tsp ground ginger

2.5ml/½ tsp ground allspice

225g/8oz/1 cup butter, melted

2 eggs, beaten

about 500g/1¼lb/5 cups plain (all-purpose) flour, plus extra for dusting

10ml/2 tsp bicarbonate of soda (baking soda)

200g/7oz white chocolate, finely grated

Cook's Tips

• You can make double the dough and freeze it in two pieces ready for when you want to bake fresh cookies.

• The baked cookies keep well in an airtight container for up to a week.

Baltic Gingerbread and White Chocolate Cookies

Chocolate and ginger are a traditional festive combination and these cookies are favourites in Estonia, Latvia and Lithuania, especially at Christmas time. You can make the dough in advance and freeze it, if you like, so it is stored ready to make quick seasonal cookies when you need them.

1 Heat the golden syrup and sugar in a pan over a medium heat, and stir constantly until the sugar has dissolved. Add the cinnamon, cloves, cardamom, ginger and allspice.

2 Add the melted butter and stir to combine. Leave to cool completely.

3 Transfer into a large bowl and add the eggs, stirring well to mix thoroughly. Gradually stir in the flour and bicarbonate of soda. Add the grated chocolate and fold in gently to combine. You should now have fairly thick dough.

4 Transfer on to a working surface and knead lightly. If the dough is too wet, add a little more flour. Cover with clear film (plastic wrap) and chill overnight.

5 Preheat the oven to 180°C/350°F/Gas 4. Line a baking sheet with baking parchment. Allow the dough to rest for 15 minutes at room temperature.

6 Roll out on a floured surface until 3mm/⅛in thick. Cut into shapes using pastry (cookie) cutters of your choice. Bake for 6–8 minutes or until golden. Leave to cool briefly on the baking sheet, then transfer to a wire rack to cool completely.

Per portion Energy 119kcal/501kJ; Protein 1.6g; Carbohydrate 17.3g, of which sugars 9.5g; Fat 5.33g, of which saturates 3.25g; Cholesterol 18mg; Calcium 30.52mg; Fibre 0.31g; Sodium 52mg.

Latvian Pancakes

Every nation has its own variation on the crêpe or pancake. This Latvian version is particularly light because the egg whites have been whisked to give the batter extra volume. The pancakes are always served with a fruit preserve.

1 Sift the flour into a bowl and add the sugar. Mix well together, then add the egg yolks and whisk to combine, using an electric whisk, if you like. Slowly add the milk, whisking constantly to make a smooth batter.

2 Add the vanilla seeds and mix again. Put the egg whites into a clean, grease-free bowl and whisk until they form stiff peaks. Gently fold into the egg batter.

3 Melt a little butter in a small frying pan or crêpe pan, over a medium heat. Pour in 120ml/4fl oz/½ cup of batter, and tilt the pan to cover the base of the pan evenly. Cook for 2–3 minutes, until golden, then turn and cook the other side. Keep warm while you make pancakes with the remaining batter. Serve the pancakes warm with preserves and sour cream.

Per portion Energy 137kcal/579kJ; Protein 4g; Carbohydrate 21.8g, of which sugars 7.2g; Fat 4.5g, of which saturates 2.4g; Cholesterol 41mg; Calcium 75mg; Fibre 0.6g; Sodium 56mg.

Serves 6

115g/4oz/1 cup plain (all-purpose) flour

30ml/2 tbsp caster (superfine) sugar

2 eggs, separated

200ml/7fl oz/scant 1 cup milk

seeds of 1 vanilla pod (bean)

20–25g/¾–1oz butter, for cooking

To serve

200g/7oz/¾ cup preserve

100ml/3½fl oz/scant ½ cup sour cream

Makes 18–20

115g/4oz/$\frac{1}{2}$ cup butter

60ml/4 tbsp caster (superfine) sugar

150g/5oz/1$\frac{1}{4}$ cups rye flour

115g/4oz/1 cup wholemeal (whole-wheat) flour

5ml/1 tsp baking powder

30ml/2 tbsp honey

1 egg white, lightly beaten

45ml/3 tbsp poppy seeds

Variation Add 100g/3$\frac{1}{4}$oz chocolate chips to the dough – chocolate and poppy seeds are a great combination.

Baltic Rye, Poppy Seed and Honey Cookies

The combination of rye, poppy seeds and honey is a classic Baltic mix of ingredients, with the poppy seeds adding a fine, nutty texture. Variations of these light cookies can be found all over the Baltic region.

1 Put the butter and sugar in a bowl and beat until creamy, using a hand mixer if you like. Sift in the flours and baking powder and combine using a wooden spoon. Add the honey and mix well. Shape the dough into a thick sausage shape about 20cm/8in long.

2 Brush the dough with the lightly beaten egg white and roll in the poppy seeds to coat. Wrap in clear film (plastic wrap) and chill for 1 hour.

3 Preheat the oven to 180°C/350°F/Gas 4 and line a large baking sheet with baking parchment. Unwrap the rolled dough and slice into 2cm/$\frac{3}{4}$in thick rounds. Arrange on the baking sheet, about 3cm/1$\frac{1}{4}$in apart, then bake for 8–10 minutes. Cool on a wire rack and store in an airtight container.

Per portion Energy 116kcal/484kJ; Protein 2g; Carbohydrate 13.7g, of which sugars 4.4g; Fat 6.3g, of which saturates 3.3g; Cholesterol 13mg; Calcium 22mg; Fibre 1.6g; Sodium 47mg.

Rye, Soda and Cream Cheese Bread

This is a slightly lighter version of the traditional soda bread eaten in Latvia.
In common with all soda breads, it does not use yeast, as bicarbonate of soda
provides the raising agent. This recipe uses cream cheese, although in Latvia a
local or homemade cottage or curd cheese would be used.

1 Preheat the oven to 180°C/350°F/Gas 4. Butter and line a 30 x 25cm/10 x 12in
loaf tin (pan). Put the cream cheese, milk and sugar into a bowl and stir well to mix.

2 Sift the flours with the bicarbonate of soda into the cream cheese mixture, then
stir in. Add the oil and mix well to combine. Pour this mixture into the prepared tin.
Bake for 25–30 minutes, or until the bread is golden in colour.

Per portion Energy 2230kcal/9341kJ; Protein 40g; Carbohydrate 251.2g, of which sugars 11.7g; Fat
125.9g, of which saturates 64.5g; Cholesterol 202mg; Calcium 661mg; Fibre 27g; Sodium 715mg.

Makes 1 loaf

200g/7oz/scant 1 cup cream cheese

200ml/7fl oz/scant 1 cup milk

5ml/1 tsp sugar

200g/7oz/1¾ cups rye flour

115g/4oz/1 cup plain (all-purpose) flour

5ml/1 tsp bicarbonate of soda
(baking soda)

30ml/2 tbsp vegetable oil

Cook's Tip For a lighter bread, replace
the given quantity of rye flour with
100g/3½oz rye flour and 100g/3½oz
wholemeal (whole-wheat) flour.

Makes 25 slices

1 litre/1½ pints/4 cups buttermilk
40g/1½oz/3 tbsp butter, melted
700g/1lb 9oz/6¼ cups barley flour
10ml/2 tsp bicarbonate of soda (baking soda)
10ml/2 tsp salt
5ml/1 tsp honey
10ml/2 tsp fennel seeds

Cook's Tip Toast this bread and serve it with honey.

Estonian Buttermilk and Fennel Seed Bread

Fennel seeds give extra spice to bread, as well as to compôtes, pickles and liqueurs. This yeast-free bread is so deliciously light and fluffy, that when eaten warm, it could easily be described as a cake. Serve it with lashings of butter.

1 Preheat the oven to 180°C/350°F/Gas 4. Grease and line a 25 x 40cm/ 10 x 16in cake tin (pan) with baking parchment. Put the buttermilk in a pan and gently heat until lukewarm, and then add the melted butter. Pour the mixture into a large bowl.

2 Sift the flour, bicarbonate of soda and salt into the bowl and stir in, then add the honey and fennel seeds and combine well.

3 Spoon the mixture into the prepared tin and bake for 25–30 minutes, or until a skewer inserted into the centre comes out clean. Serve hot with butter.

Per portion Energy 119kcal/507kJ; Protein 3.6g; Carbohydrate 23.4g, of which sugars 2.2g; Fat 2g, of which saturates 1g; Cholesterol 5mg; Calcium 57mg; Fibre 3.3g; Sodium 191mg.

Useful addresses

UK

Baltic Market
56 Ballards Lane
Finchley, London N3 2BU
Tel: +44 20 8343 1431
Grocers

Babushka
71 West Bars
Chesterfield, Derbyshire S40 1BA
Tel: +44 1246 555 336
www.babushkauk.com
*Delicatessen with multiple
locations across the UK*

Baltic Restaurant
74 Blackfriars Road, London SE1
Tel: +44 20 7928 1111

Bronek's Polski Sklep
124 Northfield Avenue
Ealing, London W13 9AB
Tel: +44 20 8579 2722
www.polskisklep.co.uk
Polish delicatessen/grocers

Costcutter
Tel: +44 1904 488663
www.costcutter.com
*Supermarket chain/retailer of
various Polish foodstuffs*

Lituanica UK Ltd
3 Gallions Close
Barking, Essex IG11 0JD
Tel: +44 208 591 5599
www.lituanica@btconnect.com

Perestroyka
242 Narborough Road,
Leicester LE3 2AP
Tel: +44 116 222 8928
Russian supermarket

Polonium Deli
300 London Road, Sheffield S2
Tel: +44 114 250 8989
www.poloniumtravel.co.uk/
polonium-deli.html

Ireland

Lituanica Warehouse
Dublin Industrial Estate,
106 Lagan Road, Glasnevin
Dublin 11
Tel: +353 1860 2380
www.lituanicaltd@yahoo.ie

Holland

Sadko
Borgergade 23, 9000 Aalborg
Tel: 96 33 00 33
Eastern European specialities

USA

'Little Lithuania' in southwest
Chicago has a high population of
Lithuanians and therefore many
delicatessens and grocers.

Baltic European Deli
632 Dorchester Avenue
Boston, MA 02127

**Continent European
Delicatessen**
5961 University Avenue #314
San Diego, CA 92115
Tel: +1 (619) 583 6366

European Food Bakery
9230 S. Hwy 17-92
Maitland, FL 32751
Tel: +1 (407) 260 9511

Food Home Inc.
PO Box 411172
Chicago, IL 60641
Tel: 312.324.0280
www.valgiai.com

Gastronom Russian Deli
5801 Geary Blvd.
San Francisco, CA 94121

**Healthy Food Lithuanian
Restaurant**
3236 South Halsted Street
Chicago, IL 60608

King of Latvia Delicatessen
1301 Ave. U, Homecrest
Brooklyn, NY 11229
Tel: +1 (718) 382 5636

Lithuanian Bakery
131 Inslee Place
Port Elizabeth, NJ 07206-2010
Tel: +1 (908) 354 0970
www.lithbake.com

Magruder's Grocery Stores
PO Box 1432
Rockville, Maryland 20849-1432
www.magruders.com

Racine Bakery
6216 West Archer Avenue
Chicago, IL 60638
www.racinebakery.com

Old Vilnius
8718 112th Street
Richmond Hill, NY 11418
Tel: +1 (718) 850 9061

Canada

**The Amber Garden and
Dalmacia Restaurant**
1702 Carling Avenue, Ottawa, ON
Tel: +1 613 728 0000

Karlik Pastry
762 Barton Street East
Hamilton, ON L8L 3B1
Tel: +1 905 544 2730

LCBO Supermarket
2180 Bloor Street West
Toronto, ON M6S 1N3
Tel: +1 416 767 8931
www.lcbo.com

Polish Food Centre
10133 Princess Elizabeth Avenue
Edmonton, AB T5G 0X9
Tel: +1 780 477 8687

Australia

Baltic Deli
Shop 1, 4 Neville Avenue
Laverton, Victoria 3028
Tel: +61 03 9369 4739
www.balticdeli.com.au

Nazdrowie Restaurant
161 Glebe Point Road
Glebe, NSW 2037
Tel: +61 02 9660 1242
www.nazdrowie.com.au

Polish Deli
Shop 5–6 Dairy Produce Hall
Victoria Market
Melbourne, Victoria 3000
www.qvm.com.au

Useful Weblinks

www.lithuanian.american.org/
duona_en.php

www.latvia-florida.org/custom3.html

www.poloniacanada.ca/services
/groceries.htm

Advice on fish sustainability

The Environmental Defense Fund
257 Park Avenue South,
New York, NY 10010
Tel: (800) 684-3322
www.edf.or

World Wildlife Fund
Tel: +41 22 364 91 11
www.panda.org

Index

Publisher's acknowledgements

The publishers would like to thank
the following for permission to
reproduce their images: p6l
istockphoto; p6r DEA/W. Buss/
Getty; p8l and p8r istockphoto;
p9t Danita Delimont/Alamy; p9bl
Sven Zacek/Alamy; p9br
istockphoto; p10 North Wind
Picture Archives/Alamy; p11l
Hulton-Deutsch Collection/
CORBIS; p11r Maria Adelaide
Silva/Alamy; p12 Jonathan Smith/
Alamy; p13t FotoIJ/Alamy; p13b
Jonathan Smith/Alamy; p14l
RigaEr/Alamy; p14r Content Mine
International/Alamy; p15tl Peter
Turnley/CORBIS; p15tr RigaYi/
Alamy; p15b Caro/Alamy; p16r
Sherab/Alamy; p17l Jonathan
Smith/Alamy; p17r Caro/Alamy;
p21tm Bon Appetit/Alamy; p21tr
Gary Woods/Alamy; p21cr
iStockphoto.
t=top, b=bottom, r=right, l=left,
m=middle. All other photographs
© Anness Publishing Ltd.